YOUNG AND JOBLESS

YOUNG AND JOBLESS

The Social and Personal Consequences of Long-term Youth Unemployment

Susan McRae

Policy Studies Institute

PSI Publications are obtainable from all good bookshops, or by visiting the Institute at 100 Park Village East, London NW1 3SR (01-387 2171)

Sales Representation: Printer Publishers Ltd
Orders to: Marston Book Services, P.O. Box 87, Oxford OX4 1LB

A CIP catalogue record of this book is available from the British Library

PS Research Report 671

ISBN 0-85374-393-2

Printed in Great Britain by T. H. Brickell & Son Ltd.,
The Blackmore Press, Longmead, Shaftesbury, Dorset.

ACKNOWLEDGEMENTS

I wish to thank both the Joseph Rowntree Memorial Trust and the Department of Employment for making this study possible. The Joseph Rowntree Memorial Trust generously funded the project, and the Department of Employment kindly allowed access to respondents from the 1984 national survey of the young unemployed. Further, I wish to thank my PSI colleagues, Dr Michael White, for his suggestions and criticisms, and Mrs Pat Gay, for carrying out the exploratory interviews for the study. Mention must also be made of the women and one man who conducted the final interviews, and the several typists who transcribed the tapes. My sincere thanks to all of them. The last thank you is reserved, of course, for the young men and women who so willingly gave their time and views to the interviewers. Without them, there would be no study.

CONTENTS

1   BEING YOUNG AND JOBLESS
     Introduction   1
     The rise of youth unemployment   1
     The 1984 survey   3
     The present study   7
     Notes   9

2   IN THE LABOUR MARKET
     Introduction   11
     Employed and unemployed   12
     The search for work   15
     The Jobcentre   17
     Jobs are important   21
     Avoiding unemployment   25
     Schemes   30
     Casual work   33
     Voluntary work   37
     Notes   38

3   QUALIFICATIONS AND TRAINING
     Introduction   39
     Qualifications and employment   40
     Staying on   41
     Training   45
     When training is wanted   50
     The highly-qualified   52
     Middle-class kids   59
     Notes   63

4 LIVING ON THE DOLE
   Introduction   64
   Money   65
   Having friends   69
   Money makes the difference   73
   Living at home   77
   Leaving home   82
   Getting married   86
   Being married   90
   Married men   91
   Married women   95
   Notes   102

5 SPECIAL DISADVANTAGES
   Introduction   103
   Ethnic minorities and racism   103
   Ill-health   107
   In trouble; in prison   116
   Notes   120

6 LIVING IN SOCIETY
   Introduction   121
   Feeling cheated   123
   Feeling angry   125
   Political perspectives   131
   The future   137
   Notes   142

7 CONCLUSIONS
   Getting jobs   143
   Living without work   146
   Getting married   147
   Futures without work?   148
   Policy implications   150

   BIBLIOGRAPHY   152

TABLES

Table 1.1   Summary of participants   8

Table 3.1   Educational qualifications of the young unemployed   40

1 BEING YOUNG AND JOBLESS

Introduction

This is a book about young men and women in long-term unemployment. Its focus is upon the social and personal consequences of living without work in a society where, despite rising and persistent unemployment, the majority of men and women have jobs. The book is not about aggregate statistical analyses of youth unemployment but is based instead upon detailed personal interviews with unemployed young men and women. In adopting a qualitative approach, the aim of the book is two-fold: first, to understand what it means to be young and without work from the perspective of the young people themselves; and second, to provide documentary evidence about the effects of prolonged joblessness, in the hope of stimulating and contributing to public debate about the problems and needs of the young unemployed. Throughout, the book relies upon the words of the young people themselves, letting them talk about their lives as they understand them. In addition, however, the book is informed by the results of sociological and policy-oriented research about unemployment. The intent is to portray, in social terms, the experiences of unemployed young men and women as they try to find work, make and keep friends, and live alone or with their parents or with husbands and wives. Further, the intent is to understand the social implications of unemployment for the position of the young unemployed in society generally, both as citizens and as future mothers and fathers of new generations of young people. Being young and jobless is, then, the focus and content of what follows. Before turning to the young unemployed, however, a brief overview of the rise of youth unemployment is given.

The rise of youth unemployment

Youth unemployment is a problem of the 1980s, a decade which has witnessed an unprecedented rise in the rate of joblessness among young people. By April 1986, more than one-third of men and women in reg-

1

istered unemployment were under the age of 25, comprising some 1.37 million young would-be workers. Over 900,000 of these young people were aged 18-24 years; one in three of them had been without work for more than one year, and one in twelve for more than three years. Youth unemployment in Britain began rising relative to total unemployment in the early 1960s, but until the mid-1970s, when rates of joblessness among young people accelerated sharply, it was not recognised as a separate problem (Casson, 1979; Ashton, 1986). However, even by the end of the 1970s youth unemployment had reached only about one-third of the level which was to be attained by the mid-1980s. And from 1982 onwards youth unemployment grew more rapidly than total unemployment, thereby increasing youth's share.

In the 1980s, therefore, the risk of unemployment became greater for young people than for others in the labour market (Sorrentino, 1980). Moreover, the risk of *long-term* youth unemployment increased. At the beginning of the decade, only about one-third of young men and women in unemployment had been out of work for six or more months; by 1984, however, joblessness of six or more months grew to include just over half of unemployed young men and just under half of unemployed young women (White and McRae, forthcoming). Furthermore, while the proportion of young men and women out of work for more than one year appears to have stabilised in the year from April 1985 to April 1986, the proportion unemployed for three or more years increased to encompass nearly 100,000 young would-be workers[1]. In addition to a doubling of total youth unemployment during the early 1980s, then, there has been a steady displacement of the young unemployed into prolonged durations of joblessness (White and McRae, forthcoming).

With the advent of rising and persistent unemployment among young people came attempts to explain its cause. As Ashton (1986) points out, such explanations were sought first in demographic changes in the composition of the working population, and later in the high wages paid to young workers. The young unemployed of the 1980s are part of the *baby boom* of the 1960s, which was largely responsible for an increase of 1.8 million in the population of working age during the years 1975-1984. However, as Ashton notes further, growth in the supply of young people to the labour market in fact peaked in 1979, before the sharp upturn in rates of youth unemployment in the early 1980s. Thus, an oversupply of young people in the labour market can be, at best, only a partial explanation of widespread youth unemployment. The suggestion that young people have priced themselves out of work as a result of changes in legislation that lowered the age for payment of adult wage rates to below age 21 was addressed by Wells (1983) in an analysis of national data spanning the years 1969-1981. Wells' study shows that the employment of young

2

posite extreme, who had never worked at all since leaving school. This group comprises 23 per cent of all men and 29 per cent of all women surveyed. But again, analysis by year of entry reveals marked differences between respondents, with only 8 per cent of men and 12 per cent of women entering between 1975 and 1979 failing to find employment in contrast to about 44 per cent of both sexes entering during the latter period.

The third group was made up of young people with intermediate work histories including a mixture of jobs of varying lengths, spells of jobless-ness and, frequently, participation in government schemes — in short, what is known as sub-employment. These young people represent the largest group within the survey: 53 per cent of the men and 47 per cent of the women. However, unlike the first two groups, only slight differences exist by year of entry into the labour market. Between the men, only one percentage point separates those entering earlier from those entering later; in contrast, more women entering during 1980-83 experienced sub-employment than did women entering during 1975-79 (54 per cent and 40 per cent respectively), reflecting the fact that more women than men entering the labour market during the earlier period had had success in establishing stable work histories.

This brief description of the three main employment patterns of the young unemployed in the 1984 survey demonstrates the difficulties fac-ing young men and women in a changing labour market. In principle at least, young people coming to the labour market with identical personal qualities or educational qualifications, or young people using identical job search techniques, could end up with markedly different work his-tories — stable employment or no employment — depending upon the period during which they sought work. Furthermore, young people with poor educational qualifications leaving school for work in the earlier pe-riod could enjoy much greater success in the labour market than young people with better educational qualifications leaving school in the later period. In other words, the changes in the youth labour market over these in and of themselves markedly affected young people's chances, independently of any individual actions or attainments.

1984 survey has been discussed in some detail in order to provide setting for the present research. Respondents to this study were from among the participants in the national survey, and thus the experiences of the young men and women of the 1984 survey are the experiences of the young people investigated here. Where, however, the emphasis of the survey was to understand the economic and la-bour behaviour of the young unemployed, the present emphasis is to understand and document the social and personal experiences of young people out work.

people under the age of 18 does appear to have been reduced by increases in their average earnings relative to average adult earnings. This decrease in employment was particularly apparent for young men. In addition, however, Wells demonstrates that the average earnings of young people relative to those of adults do not appear to have risen since the mid-1970s. Thus, high wage rates for young workers were possibly less significant in explaining rising youth unemployment at the end of the period in ques-tion than at the beginning. This possibility notwithstanding, Wells' work clearly demonstrates that high youth wage rates have contributed to the growth of youth unemployment.

There are other reasons why young people are likely to suffer dis-proportionately in times of high unemployment. Falling aggregate de-mand entails a falling off, or at the least a slowing down, of recruitment. Young people, by virtue of being new entrants to the labour market, are thus liable to have reduced chances of being hired. Last-in, first-out redundancy practices are likely to mean a further loss of jobs for young people. Moreover, in times of high overall unemployment young people will find themselves in competition for jobs with workers who have considerably more employment experience, as well as with increasing numbers of married women returning to paid employment after a break for childcare responsibilities. Unemployed 18-24 year olds will also find themselves in competition with younger and cheaper school-leavers (Sinfield, 1981). The preference of employers for recently laid-off pre-vious employees or workers with only short spells of unemployment will also aggravate the employment chances of the young unemployed (Ash-ton, 1986). The general decline in aggregate demand is, then, a necessary part of the explanation of the increase in youth unemployment. However, it is not the full explanation.

It is now widely recognised that a major shift from manual to white-collar jobs, and especially to higher level white-collar jobs, has occurred in the occupational structure in recent decades. The 1980s have, further, witnessed a sharp decline in manufacturing industries in particular. This shift has caused an imbalance between the structure of occupations and the supply of labour, with an excess of workers offering themselves for jobs in the contracting lower segments of the labour market. High and persistent rates of youth unemployment are one result (Casson, 1979; Ashton and Maguire, 1983; Roberts, 1983). The undoubted link between youth unemployment and this structural imbalance of occupations and labour supply is clearly demonstrated by the 1984 national survey of the young unemployed.

The 1984 survey
No national survey of the unemployed had taken young people as its

exclusive focus until a sample survey of approximately 2500 18-24 year olds with six or more months of continuous unemployment at the time of sampling (as defined by registration for benefit) was conducted in 1984 by the Policy Studies Institute on behalf of the Department of Employment (White and McRae, forthcoming). The primary aim of this survey was to investigate the labour market experiences of the young unemployed, with a view to understanding their behaviour as job-seekers and economic actors. Its findings give support to the contention that widespread unemployment among 18-24 year olds cannot be explained as wholly the result of rigidities in the behaviour of the young unemployed in the labour market. For example, in regard to wage rigidities, the 1984 survey not only provides evidence that real wages had been static or decreasing for this age group, but also demonstrates that no consistent relationship exists between the stated wage expectations of the young unemployed and the wages gained from jobs actually accepted. Furthermore, evidence of high levels of flexibility among the young unemployed was found in regard to both hours of work and industrial or occupational mobility. Far from showing rigidities of behaviour, the young unemployed of the 1984 survey were, if anything, too flexible in their labour market behaviour[2].

The 1984 survey does provide clear evidence, however, of the impact on young people's employment chances of a structural imbalance between occupations and labour supply; between, that is, the closure of opportunity in the lower half of the labour market and the types of jobs for which the young unemployed were offering their labour. Only a tiny minority of the young men and women in the survey had previously held higher level white-collar or clerical occupations prior to entering unemployment. Instead, 88 per cent of the men who had previously been employed had held manual or personal service jobs, and 92 per cent of the previously-employed women had held manual, personal service or junior non-manual jobs. In other words, almost all the jobs of the young unemployed had been located in the lower half of the labour market, and disproportionately so located in comparison with the representation of young workers in these occupations in the population generally[3]. Moreover, in comparison with the working population, the young unemployed were found to have worked disproportionately with employers and in industries and occupations offering relatively precarious employment. For example, the young unemployed were over-represented relative to the working population in small firms, in industries such as food and drink, clothing and footwear, hotels and catering, and in unskilled and semi-skilled positions. The problems facing the young unemployed are, then, those associated with seeking work in segments of the labour market which provide a declining proportion of total employment and

obtaining work in sectors noted for precarious employm[ent] simply, the imbalance in the youth labour market consists young people offering themselves for too few jobs in the lower half of the labour market.

The evidence of the 1984 survey regarding this imbala[nce] onstrates how unlikely it is that *individual* flexibility in labou[r] behaviour will bring employment to these unemployed young [men] women. Moreover, the young unemployed are not likely to suc[ceed in] competition for jobs in higher segments of the labour markets. The survey shows that the levels of qualification and non-qualification o[f the] young unemployed are comparable to the levels obtained by si[milar] young people in employment in the lower half of the labour market[, and] that these qualifications are not sufficient to allow them to compete [for] higher level occupations. The 1984 survey is drawn upon furthe[r in] Chapter 3 where the link between qualifications and unemployme[nt is] discussed in detail.

That the difficulties faced by the young unemployed are often be[yond] the scope of remedial *individual* action may be demonstrated furthe[r by] examining the effects year of entry into the labour market had on th[e job] chances of young people. It was noted above that although youth [un]employment rose in the mid and late 1970s, there was a sharp inc[rease] during the early 1980s. The respondents to the 1984 survey, being 18-24 years, thus entered the labour market under differing labour [mar]ket conditions, with the older respondents coming into the labour m[arket] between 1975 and 1979, and the younger between 1980 and 198[3. The] differences in rates of unemployment over these years led to [dif]ferent outcomes in the labour market for these young people [depending] upon their date of entry. The work histories of the young [people] illustrate these differing outcomes.

Respondents to the 1984 survey can generally be [placed in] broad groups. First, young people who, from the [mid] 1970s, would appear to have found secure place[s] having spent most of their time since leaving s[chool in] jobs of two to three years' duration. Almost o[ne-third of the] women in the survey as a whole come into [this group. When] the sample is disaggregated by year of e[ntry it] becomes clear that it is primarily men [entering in] 1975-79 who found stable employm[ent. These men and] women (49 per cent and 47 per ce[nt who entered the labour] market during 1975-79 had held [jobs before entering] unemployment, as compared wit[h those who entered] between 1980 and 1983.

The second group was made up o[f]

people under the age of 18 does appear to have been reduced by increases in their average earnings relative to average adult earnings. This decrease in employment was particularly apparent for young men. In addition, however, Wells demonstrates that the average earnings of young people relative to those of adults do not appear to have risen since the mid-1970s. Thus, high wage rates for young workers were possibly less significant in explaining rising youth unemployment at the end of the period in question than at the beginning. This possibility notwithstanding, Wells' work clearly demonstrates that high youth wage rates have contributed to the growth of youth unemployment.

There are other reasons why young people are likely to suffer disproportionately in times of high unemployment. Falling aggregate demand entails a falling off, or at the least a slowing down, of recruitment. Young people, by virtue of being new entrants to the labour market, are thus liable to have reduced chances of being hired. Last-in, first-out redundancy practices are likely to mean a further loss of jobs for young people. Moreover, in times of high overall unemployment young people will find themselves in competition for jobs with workers who have considerably more employment experience, as well as with increasing numbers of married women returning to paid employment after a break for childcare responsibilities. Unemployed 18-24 year olds will also find themselves in competition with younger and cheaper school-leavers (Sinfield, 1981). The preference of employers for recently laid-off previous employees or workers with only short spells of unemployment will also aggravate the employment chances of the young unemployed (Ashton, 1986). The general decline in aggregate demand is, then, a necessary part of the explanation of the increase in youth unemployment. However, it is not the full explanation.

It is now widely recognised that a major shift from manual to white-collar jobs, and especially to higher level white-collar jobs, has occurred in the occupational structure in recent decades. The 1980s have, further, witnessed a sharp decline in manufacturing industries in particular. This shift has caused an imbalance between the structure of occupations and the supply of labour, with an excess of workers offering themselves for jobs in the contracting lower segments of the labour market. High and persistent rates of youth unemployment are one result (Casson, 1979; Ashton and Maguire, 1983; Roberts, 1983). The undoubted link between youth unemployment and this structural imbalance of occupations and labour supply is clearly demonstrated by the 1984 national survey of the young unemployed.

The 1984 survey

No national survey of the unemployed had taken young people as its exclusive focus until a sample survey of approximately 2500 18-24 year olds with six or more months of continuous unemployment at the time of sampling (as defined by registration for benefit) was conducted in 1984 by the Policy Studies Institute on behalf of the Department of Employment (White and McRae, forthcoming). The primary aim of this survey was to investigate the labour market experiences of the young unemployed, with a view to understanding their behaviour as job-seekers and economic actors. Its findings give support to the contention that widespread unemployment among 18-24 year olds cannot be explained as wholly the result of rigidities in the behaviour of the young unemployed in the labour market. For example, in regard to wage rigidities, the 1984 survey not only provides evidence that real wages had been static or decreasing for this age group, but also demonstrates that no consistent relationship exists between the stated wage expectations of the young unemployed and the wages gained from jobs actually accepted. Furthermore, evidence of high levels of flexibility among the young unemployed was found in regard to both hours of work and industrial or occupational mobility. Far from showing rigidities of behaviour, the young unemployed of the 1984 survey were, if anything, too flexible in their labour market behaviour[2].

The 1984 survey does provide clear evidence, however, of the impact on young people's employment chances of a structural imbalance between occupations and labour supply; between, that is, the closure of opportunity in the lower half of the labour market and the types of jobs for which the young unemployed were offering their labour. Only a tiny minority of the young men and women in the survey had previously held higher level white-collar or clerical occupations prior to entering unemployment. Instead, 88 per cent of the men who had previously been employed had held manual or personal service jobs, and 92 per cent of the previously-employed women had held manual, personal service or junior non-manual jobs. In other words, almost all the jobs of the young unemployed had been located in the lower half of the labour market, and disproportionately so located in comparison with the representation of young workers in these occupations in the population generally[3]. Moreover, in comparison with the working population, the young unemployed were found to have worked disproportionately with employers and in industries and occupations offering relatively precarious employment. For example, the young unemployed were over-represented relative to the working population in small firms, in industries such as food and drink, clothing and footwear, hotels and catering, and in unskilled and semi-skilled positions. The problems facing the young unemployed are, then, those associated with seeking work in segments of the labour market which provide a declining proportion of total employment and obtaining work in sectors noted for precarious employment. To put it simply, the imbalance in the youth labour market consists in too many young people offering themselves for too few jobs in the contracting lower half of the labour market.

The evidence of the 1984 survey regarding this imbalance demonstrates how unlikely it is that *individual* flexibility in labour market behaviour will bring employment to these unemployed young men and women. Moreover, the young unemployed are not likely to succeed in competition for jobs in higher segments of the labour markets. The 1984 survey shows that the levels of qualification and non-qualification of the young unemployed are comparable to the levels obtained by similar young people in employment in the lower half of the labour market, but that these qualifications are not sufficient to allow them to compete for higher level occupations. The 1984 survey is drawn upon further in Chapter 3 where the link between qualifications and unemployment is discussed in detail.

That the difficulties faced by the young unemployed are often beyond the scope of remedial *individual* action may be demonstrated further by examining the effects year of entry into the labour market had on the job chances of young people. It was noted above that although youth unemployment rose in the mid and late 1970s, there was a sharp increase during the early 1980s. The respondents to the 1984 survey, being aged 18-24 years, thus entered the labour market under differing labour market conditions, with the older respondents coming into the labour market between 1975 and 1979, and the younger between 1980 and 1983. The differences in rates of unemployment over these years led to very different outcomes in the labour market for these young people, depending upon their date of entry. The work histories of the young unemployed illustrate these differing outcomes.

Respondents to the 1984 survey can generally be divided into three broad groups. First, young people who, from the vantage point of the 1970s, would appear to have found secure places in the labour market, having spent most of their time since leaving school in work and holding jobs of two to three years' duration. Almost one-quarter of both men and women in the survey as a whole come into this group. When, however, the sample is disaggregated by year of entry into the labour market, it becomes clear that it is primarily men and women entering work during 1975-79 who found stable employment. Almost half of both men and women (49 per cent and 47 per cent respectively) entering the labour market during 1975-79 had held stable jobs prior to entering long-term unemployment, as compared with only 2 per cent of both sexes entering between 1980 and 1983.

The second group was made up of young men and women at the opposite extreme, who had never worked at all since leaving school. This group comprises 23 per cent of all men and 29 per cent of all women surveyed. But again, analysis by year of entry reveals marked differences between respondents, with only 8 per cent of men and 12 per cent of women entering between 1975 and 1979 failing to find employment in contrast to about 44 per cent of both sexes entering during the latter period.

The third group was made up of young people with intermediate work histories including a mixture of jobs of varying lengths, spells of joblessness and, frequently, participation in government schemes — in short, what is known as sub-employment. These young people represent the largest group within the survey: 53 per cent of the men and 47 per cent of the women. However, unlike the first two groups, only slight differences exist by year of entry into the labour market. Between the men, only one percentage point separates those entering earlier from those entering later; in contrast, more women entering during 1980-83 experienced sub-employment than did women entering during 1975-79 (54 per cent and 40 per cent respectively), reflecting the fact that more women than men entering the labour market during the earlier period had had success in establishing stable work histories.

This brief description of the three main employment patterns of the young unemployed in the 1984 survey demonstrates the difficulties facing young men and women in a changing labour market. In principle at least, young people coming to the labour market with identical personal qualities or educational qualifications, or young people using identical job search techniques, could end up with markedly different work histories — stable employment or no employment — depending upon the period during which they sought work. Furthermore, young people with poor educational qualifications leaving school for work in the earlier period could enjoy much greater success in the labour market than young people with better educational qualifications leaving school in the later period. In other words, the changes in the youth labour market over these years in and of themselves markedly affected young people's chances, independently of any individual actions or attainments.

The 1984 survey has been discussed in some detail in order to provide the setting for the present research. Respondents to this study were drawn from among the participants in the national survey, and thus the experiences of the young men and women of the 1984 survey are the experiences of the young people investigated here. Where, however, the primary emphasis of the survey was to understand the economic and labour market behaviour of the young unemployed, the present emphasis is to understand and document the social and personal experiences of young people without work.

The present study

The 1984 survey provides an aggregate picture and analysis of young people in unemployment; as such, it illuminates our understanding about which young people enter into long-term unemployment, where and why they do so. This is the ultimate aim of survey research. However, aggregate analyses shed little light — nor are they intended to — on how young people experience unemployment as individuals. Therefore, the data for the present study come from tape-recorded, in-depth interviews with young men and women in unemployment and focus, *inter alia,* upon employment-related issues such as job preferences and dislikes, looking for work, attitudes towards the Jobcentre; upon personal relations within unemployment, including friends, parents and partners if married or living as married; upon expectations for the future, including getting married and having children as well as future prospects for employment; upon attitudes towards unemployment; and upon wider political and social views.

Research for the project began at the end of 1985 when 40 exploratory interviews were carried out with respondents to the 1984 survey living in Gosport, Oxford, London and Wolverhampton. These initial interviews were almost wholly unstructured and contributed significantly to the development of the final interview schedule. For the main study, it was originally hoped to achieve 150 interviews with respondents equally divided between two northern and two southern cities. This geographical division was chosen in the hope of obtaining interviews with young people with contrasting labour market experiences. In the event, however, two developments intervened to reduce the availability of respondents to the 1984 survey for re-interview. First, a postal questionnaire follow-up was conducted in October 1985 which included about 1000 young men and women from the initial survey. It was decided not to include these among the group sought for qualitative interviewing which would have involved a third contact. Secondly, the interval between the first interviews of the young men and women in May/June 1984 and the attempt to locate them for the present study between February and May 1986 meant that many had moved house and hence could not be contacted. As a result of these two developments, an ultimate research group comprising 119 young people living in Manchester and Sheffield in the North, and London and Southampton in the South was achieved.

A second initial intention was to talk to as many women as men even though there are twice as many men as women among the registered young long-term unemployed. This balance was not ultimately achieved, however, largely because of the small number of women in the South who could be found for interviews. Women from ethnic minority groups are particularly under-represented. Only one woman of Asian origin was in-

7

cluded in the original Manchester sample (excluding those contacted in the postal follow-up), and this woman was re-interviewed for the present study. No women from ethnic minority groups were available from the original Sheffield sample, while the ten women of Asian or Afro-Caribbean origin in London and Southampton could not be located for interviews. Table 1.1 below summarises the sex, ethnic minority group and geographical location of the young men and women interviewed.

Table 1.1   Summary of participants

City	Male	Female	numbers All
Manchester	23 (2)[1]	19 (1)	42 (3)
Sheffield	22 (–)	13 (–)	35 (–)
London	19 (7)	3 (–)	22 (7)
Southampton	12 (2)	8 (–)	20 (2)
Total	76 (11)	43 (1)	119 (12)

[1] The numbers in brackets refer to the numbers of young people of Asian or Afro-Caribbean origin included in the numbers interviewed in each city.

Two further points need to be made about the selection of young people for this study. First, respondents from the 1984 survey living in London proved particularly difficult to locate, with only 8 men and 3 women of those interviewed in London being contacted as a result of their participation in the 1984 survey. The remaining 11 men (5 of West Indian origin; 6 white) were contacted outside Jobcentres in Woolwich and Camden. Analysis of the interviews of these 11 young men reveals no systematic differences between them and other respondents, however. Secondly, the participants in this study are young people who had either continued to live with their families or remained in contact with their parents, or had not moved house since the initial survey. As a result, unemployed young people living in squats or otherwise in unsettled accommodation and those who had broken relations with their families or moved away for other reasons are not included. There are few ways in which it is possible to overcome such exclusions, even though it results in a failure to cover the complete range of being young and unemployed. In a small study such as the present one, however, focusing upon a relatively well-defined group of participants can be an advantage. The loss entailed by the exclusion of some part of the full experience of unemployment among young people is more than balanced by the focused analyses which flow from concentration upon a particular group of young people.

These, then, are the young unemployed men and women discussed in the study. As noted earlier, the method of research is qualitative. The numbers are too few for any other approach. Thus, although attention is paid throughout to variations in experiences and behaviour between men and women, and between the North and South, the primary method of analysis is though the words of the young people themselves. Proportions and percentage distributions, where reported, are used only in a descriptive sense, to give some idea of broad groupings within the young unemployed and should not be interpreted as precise statistical distributions of behaviour. What is at issue is not simply how many do what, but rather the range and variety of responses of young people to life without work.

The study is divided into five chapters. Chapter 2 investigates the experiences of the young unemployed in the labour market, both in the past and currently. Here the emphasis is upon the search for work and upon the importance of work for young men and women without jobs. Paid work outside the formal labour market is also discussed. Chapter 3 investigates the relationship between qualifications and unemployment, focusing in particular upon the expectations and beliefs of the young unemployed about the value and efficacy of qualifications and training. Chapter 4 explores ways of living on the dole by documenting the consequences of unemployment for personal relationships. Here the young unemployed and their friends, parents and partners if married or living as married, are discussed. Chapter 5 analyses young men and women with special disadvantages. Experiences of racial discrimination in the labour market are discussed, as well as the consequences of physical and psychological ill-health and of being in trouble with the police. Chapter 6 documents the social and political perspectives of the young unemployed, looking at the explanations they provide for their own unemployment together with their reactions to joblessness in a society where the majority have jobs. The study ends with some general conclusions and implications for public policy.

Notes

1. Direct comparability with previous years' estimates of long-term unemployment is not possible because of changes made to the compilation of unemployment statistics. However, the Labour Market Quarterly Report, June 1986, suggests that there appears to have been a modest decline in unemployment among young people under 25 over the year from April 1985 to April 1986.

2. The 1984 survey addresses the issue of flexibility in two ways: flexibility in working hours and flexibility in industrial and occupational mobility. In relation to the first of these, working part-time could constitute one means through which young people could be drawn back into the labour market. The survey demonstrates considerable flexibility among the young unemployed towards working hours, but shows also that this flexibility did not give young people a competitive advantage in their search for work in that those young people who concentrated exclusively on full-time hours were marginally more successful in finding work than those who considered part-time as well as full-time employment. Similarly, findings from the 1984 survey suggest that there might well be conditions under which young workers demonstrate too much industrial and occupational flexibility. The rates of industrial and occupational mobility among survey respondents were exceptionally high, with the majority of those who had held more than one job experiencing changes of both industry and occupation. The idea of excessive flexibility may be based upon considerations of human capital. Training may tend to be concentrated in the first job after leaving school or, at least, in the first few jobs. Subsequent moves to jobs in different industries or occupations may fail either to utilise previous training or to provide new training. Hence, not only may previous training be wasted but performance in new jobs may be inadequate because of lack of relevant training and experience, thus exposing the young worker to increased risk of job loss. The 1984 survey found that the extent of training received by young people in their most important jobs had no bearing on their chances of finding new jobs from unemployment. Prior training appears to be disregarded by employers in selecting for vacancies, except when accompanied by a recognised qualification.

3. *The General Household Survey 1979* shows the following occupational distribution of workers aged 20-29; the relevant proportion of 1984 survey respondents are given in brackets. Men in Manual/Personal service occupations: 63% (88%); Women in Manual/Personal service/Junior Non-manual: 78% (92%). Table 6.5, *GHS* 1979, *OPCS*, HMSO, 1981.

2   IN THE LABOUR MARKET

Introduction

In Chapter 1 the nature and structure of youth unemployment in the 1980s was summarised. There it was shown that, although many of the young people now experiencing long-term unemployment once enjoyed relatively stable employment, and many others failed entirely to gain any employment beyond occasional government schemes, the largest group of young unemployed in the 1980s are men and women whose work histories comprise a mixture of jobs, government work-schemes and spells of unemployment. Varying degrees of sub-employment, in other words, have been the typical experience. However, with the passage of time, bringing increased pressure on fewer job vacancies caused in part by entry into the labour market of a fresh supply of school-leavers every year, and increased durations of personal joblessness, even short-term employment has become difficult for many young adults to obtain. By the time the respondents came to participate in the present study, *unemployment* rather than sub-employment had become the dominant labour-market experience for the majority of the young men and many of the young women.

When interviewed, nearly three-quarters of the young men and almost half of the young women had experienced five or more years of unemployment, in spells of varying durations, since leaving school. One in five of the young men had never worked other than on government-sponsored schemes; 4 young women had never worked at all. Some young people included here are, of course, continuing to find work intermittently. For these, the successful, participation in the labour market primarily comprises seeking, finding, losing and replacing a series of usually low-paid and low-skilled jobs. For the rest, however, the labour market consists essentially of trips to the Jobcentre, where the fortunate ones find short-term government-created jobs. A few undertake work outside the formal labour market; fewer still undertake unpaid work. Successful participation in the labour market is the experience of only the smallest

11

minority of the young people selected for study here. For the majority, participation in the labour market is participation in unemployment.

This chapter documents the labour market experiences of these young unemployed men and women through their own words, focusing in turn ,on the search for work, its importance, and on work outside formal employment, including participation in government schemes and casual work. As throughout, the aim is to make sense of the world which confronts these unemployed young men and women and to render intelligible their actions within that world. Perhaps the most surprising aspect of the behaviour of these young people, given the predominance of unemployment in their lives, is their continued search for work. Understanding this search forms the focus of the analysis. The chapter will conclude with a brief discussion of young people and work in the informal sector. We begin, however, with the employment status of the young people of this study at the time of interviewing, illustrating the experience of unemployment.

Employed and unemployed

All but 20 of the 119 young men and women interviewed had held paid jobs at some time since leaving school. As noted above, however, all too often these jobs were short-lived:

> I got a job before I left school as an apprentice motor mechanic. I served my apprenticeship for four year, and after the four year were up, they got rid of me. They made me redundant. Then I went to (firm) as a motor mechanic. They made me redundant because they were part of Bentley group which folded up. After that I was at (firm), they made me redundant, and then I was unemployed for a year and a half — something like that. Then I got a job at (firm) for six month and they laid me off. And I'm unemployed at present. *(Martin, Sheffield)*

> How many jobs have I had? Three. It is six years since I have left school now. Three jobs, four years on the dole. It doesn't sound good. A bloke I am working with at the moment has had three jobs so far and has only left school for a year. It is absolutely ridiculous. He was a bit more lucky than I was. *(Steve, Southampton)*

At the time of the interviews, only 10 men were in employment, in addition to 9 men employed on the Community Programme (CP) scheme. Only 6 men were in permanent jobs with some hope of employment continuing into the future. There were few differences between the young men in the North and the South, except that men in the North who were in work at the time of interviewing were more often in government-sponsored jobs than were men in the South. For many of the men, however, the experience of finding even short-term jobs seemed to have come to an end. Over half of those in unemployment when interviewed had spent more than three years in their latest spell of unemployment, and one in five of these had been without work for the previous five or more years. At the time of the interviews, only 7 men without work had been out of the labour force for less than one year. Thus, although youth unemployment is sometimes thought to be only a phase through which many young people pass, for this group at least, unemployment appears to be chronic.

For the young women, the picture appears slightly less bleak. Nearly half of the women were in paid work when interviewed: 15 in the North and 3 in the South. No women were employed on government schemes, and only 4 women in the North considered their present jobs to be temporary. In addition, 4 women were not able to seek or to do paid work owing to childcare responsibilities. The small number of women in the South (11) included in the study makes detailed geographical comparisons inappropriate.

> I've got an interview next week for another job I've applied for. It's funny — you do find that when you're employed you get more interviews than when you're not, 'cos your experience is continuous. It's more money — quite a lot more money — and it looks a nice job. But, you know, I don't tell anybody at work — they don't know any different, so if I don't get it then I've not lost anything — but if I do get it then I'll be pleased with meself. *(Fiona, Manchester)*

> Yeah, I'm working part-time. It is that record shop where I first started on a six-month scheme. It's under a year that I've been working, 'cos I started working Saturdays, you see, and then after that somebody left and I started, you know — I don't know, it's about six months, say seven months . . . Unemployed? I'd say just over a year. Wait a minute. About five months before I got that six month scheme, then I did that, then it were, like, from April to the following Christmas, or just after that. *(Liz, Sheffield)*

As well as being apparently more successful than men in finding work, the women generally had accumulated fewer years of unemployment. As the majority of them were unmarried, this difference is not accounted for by periods of non-registration as unemployed[1]. Altogether, nearly half of the women had experienced over five years' unemployment in total, with those who entered the labour market during 1980-83 somewhat more likely than those entering earlier to have spent more years out of work than in work. In contrast, three-quarters of the men had accumulated more than five years' unemployment, with few differences by year of entry into the labour market. Among those women in unemployment at the time of interviews, however, one in five had current spells of joblessness comparable to the five or more years without work experienced by the men. More than half of the women in unemployment at interviews had been without work for three or more years. And so, like the men, it seems that for many of these unemployed young women, even short-term jobs have become scarce.

Despite these few differences between men and women, it is clear that for both sexes the overwhelming fact of life in their labour market has been unemployment, broken for some by spells of work, unbroken for others since once holding work. And for 20 young men and women, employment (other than occasional government schemes for some) has been missing altogether.

> I did a business studies course, you see. Got a diploma in that so I thought that would be perfect if I got an office job . . . I thought, I've got a qualification, now what's stopping me. But I was unsuccessful, you know, when I tried for a few jobs and obviously they wanted someone with higher qualifications. I did only about 40-50 words a minute in typing. They wanted 80-100 and all the shorthand, audio-typist. [So] I went to Bolton College and I took further qualification as secretarial again and I did apply for all the jobs and again I wasn't successful . . . Unemployed altogether? Five years now. *(Fatima, Manchester)*

> I had an interview and everything — he found out that I had asthma, he didn't want to know me afterwards. Then I told Careers and she put me on to these YTS schemes. I went on a few of them, then when I were 18 she said I'd have to find it through Jobcentres, that way, because she couldn't help me anymore. I expected it to be a few months after leaving school. I left when I was 16, I'm 22 now and I've been on a few schemes but . . . *(Alan, Sheffield)*

The 20 young people in the study who had yet to find their first jobs comprised 16 young men, including 11 who had participated in various goverment schemes, and 4 young women, including one who had spent five weeks on a Youth Opportunities Scheme. Only 4 (all men) of the 20 lived in the South: one in London and 3 in Southampton, confirming the greater difficulty facing young people in the North of finding even short-term employment. The experiences of many of these twenty are discussed in greater detail in subsequent chapters; at this point it should simply be noted that for these twenty, unemployment was not just a recurring feature of their participation in the labour market. It was the only feature.

The Search for work

Interviewer: What is it about looking for work that you don't like? Oh, I don't know. I suppose it's going through the same old routine: finding a job, then going for an interview, building your hopes up and then not getting it. *(Joan, Manchester)*

The unemployed young men and women of this study dislike looking for work. Neither differences of sex nor of area separate the respondents in this regard: over 70 per cent of the men and almost 80 per cent of the women in both North and South did not enjoy, or found discouraging, the search for jobs. And yet, they continue to look. The main reason for the dislike of job hunting, as suggested above, was the disappointment associated with lack of success. At least one-third of both men and women spoke of *getting turned down* as the aspect of looking for work which was the most discouraging:

I went for an interview, and I thought I'd got a really good chance of this job because I'd done everything that they required for this job, and then I got a letter saying that I wasn't — that I hadn't been accepted. And that really — I think I suppose I built me hopes up too much on it, but it — when that letter come it were like somebody dropping a weight on you. It really knocks you out. *(Martin, Sheffield)*

Being told 'No'. When you were out of a job and you got the letter — just the letters when they come through the door, they said: 'I'm sorry, it's been filled'. That was depressing . . . I thought: 'What've I done? What did I do wrong? Was I not nicely dressed or what — was my hair a mess or was it wrong?' Yes, you do feel as if it was just your fault and nobody else got rejected. You don't think that there are probably a hundred people going for that job, and ninety-nine probably feel the same. *(Fiona, Manchester)*

Getting one's hopes up but not fulfilled; blaming oneself; not understanding why it was not you that was chosen: all these were cited repeatedly by the young people of this study. A few found being turned down so discouraging that they considered not being interviewed better than having the interview but not the job. Others developed ways of coping with continuing the search for work in the face of repeated rejections:

If there's three or four there [at an interview] I feel rejected, but mostly you know you're not the only one. Sometimes there are ten jobs and 100 people apply, so you know you've got a fair chance of being rejected. Now when I apply for a job I think; 'If I get it, I'll be really lucky, but I doubt I will get it'; so if I get it then it will be a surprise. I used to think: 'I'm bound to get this one'; and then you don't get it.

You feel an idiot because you've convinced yourself you're going to get it. *(Irene, Southampton)*

I've never had a second interview on any job. It's only been the first one and then within a few days, either you get a letter or you never hear anything again ... Well, you sort of feel disheartened at first, but when you've sort of been out of work that long, you don't really care. You just say: 'Oh well, another rotten old sausage behind his desk! Go on to the next one.' *(Bernie, Southampton)*

There are other reasons behind the dislike these young men and women share about job hunting: waiting for employers to let you know the results of an interview or application and never hearing; being one of countless hundreds applying for too few jobs; filling in endless forms and answering the same questions again and again; missing out because of being too old or too young for that particular job; failing to find any job at all to apply for; and, of course, spending precious money on looking, applying and being interviewed only to find someone else got the job:

I get annoyed and I get upset sometimes because I think, 'Well I'm 23 and I've got no job, now that's not very nice'. Because, of course, you apply for a pile more jobs, it'll cost you a pile more money in envelopes and letters and stamps for application forms and bus fares and this, that and the other, and you get more depressed because you've got no money in the end and so you get nowhere. *(Adam, Manchester)*

Interviewer: What is it about looking for work that you dislike? Well, the travelling expenses more than anything. Just going to and from the interviews and not getting anything from them. *(Eileen, Manchester)*

About half of both men and women reported finding job hunting expensive, although less than one-third found that lack of money interfered with their search for work. Only slight differences by region seem to exist in respect of this issue, with Londoners somewhat more likely to complain of the costs of public transportation. Sometimes parents were able to help with the costs of looking for work. However, given that unemployment frequently runs in families, this was not always the case, as the contrasting experiences of the following young women from Manchester illustrate:

Interviewer: Did lack of money ever make it difficult for you to look for work? No, because I've got a good Mum. *(Eileen, Manchester)*

Me Dad's unemployed as well, you see, so I've found that hard [looking for work] sometimes. *Interviewer: Would you say that you've missed interviews because of the lack of money?* Yes, lots of times. *(Sue, Manchester)*

Moreover, as unemployment continues over the years rather than over a few months, the costs entailed in going for interviews multiply, sometimes to the extent that they hinder the search for work quite markedly, as this Sheffield man related:

> *Interviewer: What is it that you dislike?* Attending interviews now, because I don't have the drive. I've still got incentive but it's just I know that there's loads of people that are going to be at that interview as well, and now I've been on t'dole four years, I can't present meself like — I don't wear a suit anymore. There's absolutely no chance I can get a suit and like all these things they add up you know, they all hold you back . . . it means going round all me friends and rounding up a decent pair of shoes and a good — you know — everything. It would cost me money if I was going to buy suits, but I mean, I've got to the stage now where I'm not going to do it, it's not me priority now. I'd really like to go and get a hair cut, know what I mean? but it's only like, trimming. *(John, Sheffield)*

However, despite the cost of looking for work, and the many disappointments and aggravations of the search, only 5 men and one woman reported having stopped looking altogether, primarily as a result of discouragement. Friends and relatives were often used as sources of information about possible vacancies, as well as the newspapers. One young man advised others in the same predicament to tell everyone they met that they were looking for work: that way, something was bound to turn up eventually. But for the majority of both men and women, the Jobcentre was the main focus of job hunting. This often seems to be the case with the long-term unemployed. The Jobcentre is an impersonal institution; going there again and again involves few of the social costs attendant upon continually confronting personal acquaintances with the fact of one's persistent lack of employment. In addition, a trip to the Jobcentre is a concrete expression of the desire to work: friends, neighbours — and more importantly perhaps, parents — can see for themselves that you are at least *trying* to find a job.

The Jobcentre

Respondents to the initial 1984 survey of the young unemployed were asked about their methods of looking for work. Of those who were seeking employment when interviewed (87 per cent of the present group), about 90 per cent used Jobcentres for this purpose, with men slightly more likely to do so than women. At the time of the present research, some 18 to 24 months later, nearly three-quarters of both men and women continued to visit the Jobcentre, with few differences by area. Only 16 men (11 in the North and 5 in the South) and 6 women (3 in each area) had given up the Jobcentre entirely, despite going there when first unemployed. The frequency of visits to these centres varies of course. At each extreme — going every day and going only when signing on — there were about 10 per cent of both sexes. Young people in the North go slightly more often than in the South, with approximately one in three Northern men and women going weekly or twice-weekly compared to one in five Southerners. And about 10 per cent vary the regularity of their trips to the Jobcentre, sometimes as a way of keeping interest in the search for work:

> I'd go through periods, a week or so, where I'd go every day of the week, and sometimes I would go once a month, keep it as irregular as possible to avoid disappointments and getting bored of the whole thing. . . . Yeah, it gives me a boost during the week. I feel as if, well, I've gone to the Jobcentre. I've made some effort at least. I may not find nothing but . . . *(Terry, London)*

Often, as the above quotation suggests, going to the Jobcentre is simply an act undertaken to keep one's spirits up; it is a statement to oneself: *I am looking.* Certainly, it is rarely undertaken with much expectation of finding work. The experience of the following London man is almost unique in the present study:

> I tried all different ways of really going about it . . . I found that, I think in the end I found that [the Jobcentre] was the best way to find a job, you know. When you wrote to people, sometimes you'd never get a reply from them sort of thing, and you ring up and things, and so I think the Jobcentre was the best way of doing it, really. *(Ken, London)*

However, more common, in the present research at least, were complaints, aggravations, and disappointments. Unemployed young men and women might go to the Jobcentre, but they did not like it there, and they rarely found jobs there. It was, in fact, the lack of appropriate jobs on offer which was the most common complaint made against the Jobcentre by the young people of this study.

> It's a joke — I've been in every day for months and not seen one single job that's any good at all . . . *(Ted, Sheffield)*

> . . . it seems as though there's usually a catch with the jobs that end up in the Jobcentre . . . they seem substandard. *(Brian, Sheffield)*

Forty per cent of both men and women, North and South, spoke against the type of jobs available through the Jobcentre, with low-paid work ranking high among their complaints:

> I said to them [the Jobcentre] 'Have you got anything?' And he give me

jobs and he looked up some job, I mean, it's not being funny or anything, once I went up there and I looked at a job and they said: 'Oh this
is the ideal job, nice job'. And I said, how much is the money and they
said eighty pounds. I said how can you give me a job for eighty
pounds? I've got a wife and three kids. Now, how could they offer me a
job like that? Fair enough for a single man, yes, glad to take it on, but
not when you've got kids and that. I was getting more on the dole,
wasn't I? *(Baljit, Southampton)*

Last couple of months I haven't been going regular at all. Because, I
mean, some of the jobs there, you're getting employers taking liberties
now, offering cheap wages, because they know now that people are
really out of work, so they — it's a source of cheap labour really. *(Leroy,
London)*

However, even when jobs of some interest or paying a reasonable wage
are listed, many of these unemployed young people find that they are
either too young or too old to apply, or that they do not have the right
qualifications, skills or experience. One of the worst frustrations related
again and again, was finding a job on the board for which you were the
right age, had the right qualifications or skills, which paid a decent wage
— and which had been filled some days or weeks ago:

More often than not you'll see a job on the board — like happened to
me the last few times I've seen jobs on the board and I've gone to the
desk — 'Oh, they've been taken three days'. They never take the jobs
off the board, they've left them on. So, of course, that depresses you
because you lose faith in them. So you've about as much chance as a
poke in the eye — it's useless. *(Adam, Manchester)*

You can get a lot of interviews from the Centre but I find that when
you get there, a lot of the time the job's gone anyway, that sort of thing,
with the Jobcentre when you get there a lot of them have gone. *(Sue,
Manchester)*

Whatever the reasons for jobs which have been filled remaining on the
boards as available, such occurrences only add to the many disappointments that the young unemployed already suffer during their search for
work.

It should be noted that one-quarter of these young men and women
considered that the staff at Jobcentres were helpful, or at least tried to be
helpful. Their major complaints were not usually directed at Jobcentre
staff, and a few respondents mentioned the difficult circumstances facing
workers in these centres, given the large numbers seeking work. Sometimes, however, the fact that staff are over-loaded with applicants and

under stress means that less assertive young people miss out in the search for work. Shyness and lack of confidence, for example, hindered the efforts of the following two young men:

> *Interviewer: Did you go to the Jobcentre very often?* When I can. Maybe once a week . . . I used to look at the cards. I didn't use to bother the people who was sitting at the desks. Maybe I was scared of them. *Did you ever find any jobs when you looked at the cards?* Yes, I did — joinery and that. *Did you ever approach the people at the desk with them?* Well, I tried to but I just failed. *(Richard, Manchester)*

> *Interviewer: Do you find that the Jobcentre has been any help to you?* They didn't seem to ask about if I had any problems about looking for work or anything like that — just said what would you like to do, that's it, take away these and they left it at that. They left it all up to me, and I'm not very good on my own. *(Brian, Sheffield)*

Previous research has shown that job hunting can be demoralising (Taylor 1983:46) and that it becomes harder as time passes (EIU, 1982:78). The difficulties encountered at the Jobcentre as related by the young people of this research substantiate these earlier studies. Inadequate attention from staff, inadequate jobs, inadequate responses from employers: all of these make the search for work that much harder. Some young people give up the search entirely, others just give up the Jobcentre:

> I did, but I don't go anymore. I know there's nothing there. Everybody wants people with experience and the minute you go there, if you've been out of work for three years, they are not interested. I don't find it very helpful. *(Jane, London)*

> I have done but I don't use it now. The interviewers at the Jobcentre put you off the job before you go for it. They say, 'Are you sure you can do it? They want so many qualifications and you haven't got it all'. They don't give you a chance to go and explain yourself, they say you're not good enough, forget it. So I don't bother with them neither. *(Frank, London)*

These two young people were, however, in the minority. As stated earlier, all but 5 men and one woman in our study were continuing their search for employment, despite decreasing chances of success with increasing durations of unemployment. Furthermore, almost three-quarters of both men and women continued to use the Jobcentre in their search, despite widespread belief in the unlikeliness of finding jobs in this way. Given the beliefs and experiences of the young people of this study, it would not have been particularly surprising to discover that the majority, and not the minority, had in fact stopped looking for work, stopped using the Jobcentre. What is surprising is the fact that they continue. In the next section, an attempt is made to explain this fact.

Jobs are important

It has been suggested that a minimum standard of rationality is to abandon lines of approach that repeatedly fail; and that, rationally, to ask someone to do something for you implies, first, that it can be done and, second, that it can be done by the person requested (Jarvie, 1984). On this view, the attempts of young men and women in long-term unemployment, living in a society with more than 3 million unemployed, to find jobs through their local Jobcentres could be construed as irrational. If job hunting is expensive, demoralising and unsuccessful, and if the Jobcentre is seen as inadequate and never has appropriate jobs in any event — why keep looking there for work? Surely to do so is indeed irrational, or at best, illogical.

The young people of this study were clearly neither irrational nor illogical, however. Two partial explanations of their continuing to look for work, despite the disappointments and aggravations they encounter, have already been suggested. First, many respondents had themselves found jobs in the past, or people known to them had found jobs, often through the Jobcentre. Secondly, continuing the search for employment is a way of avoiding the accusation of laziness, of avoiding being called a *dole-scrounger*, whether by a parent, a friend or oneself:

> I mean it's not as if I'm not looking for a job because I am. I'm starting to wake up now. So as far as that's concerned I'm looking harder — I'm not just — what worries me is that you're expected as being unemployed not to look for work and that you are a lazy load of sods and that's not true. As far as I know it's not true anyway. People do want to work. *(Paul, London)*

> You get the odd spiteful comment off people: 'You don't do anything anyway', frequent one — and then: 'What do you know about it? You don't know anything anyway, only a half a day at work'. Okay, fair enough, but it's not necessarily my fault that I'm out of work — nor that I don't work; I try . . . I had spells where I didn't bother, 'cos I thought: 'Well, I'm not going to get one anyway' . . . [but] sometimes I had spells where I went all the time, and other times I'd go every fortnight — so, I did try. *(Fiona, Manchester)*

But however salient these two reasons are, it is nonetheless the importance of having a job which seems to be the primary motivation. Given the overwhelming part unemployment had played so far in the lives of these young men and women, it would not perhaps have been

21

surprising if they had come to downgrade the importance of having a job. After all, a great many of them had spent more time out of the labour force since leaving school than in paid employment. But, in fact, the majority of both men and women regard having a job as very important, not only to individuals in general but to themselves personally. Employment is seen as preventing boredom and depression; as increasing feelings of self-esteem and improving credibility in the eyes of others. Employment brings money, and with money opportunities for independence and freedom from parental restrictions. Employment means a place in society:

> I think a work environment is very important. I didn't used to think it was. In today's society anyway, when the majority of people work — I'm not a conformist but it's best to conform to that standard. You can appreciate other people's problems and appreciate the fact that people are tired when they come home from work, things like that. Plus you get a lot of fulfillment from work, or you can do if you get the right job. If I had a job now I'd be much happier. *(Brian, Sheffield)*

> I used to think that unemployment only lasts a while, everybody gets a job sooner or later. But you see people who haven't got a job sooner or later, so they haven't got a car and they haven't got a house. They haven't got anything. It's not that I won't have a car, it's that I haven't got a job. They don't allow you any self-respect. They're not bothered. You need your self-respect, it's not the respect of other people. *(Irene, Southampton)*

Perhaps unexpectedly, the importance of having employment appears to have been felt most strongly by the young women of the study. Virtually all the women attached importance to having a job, and endorsed all the reasons for doing so — importance to oneself in feeling worthwhile, useful; preventing boredom; and preventing depression. Only one woman thought that having a job was unimportant, one was uncertain, and one felt employment was more important for men than for women. Quite clearly, the times when employment could be assumed to mean more to young men than to young women seem to have passed[2], at least for these young unemployed women:

> I enjoy working — more so now than ever because I've been unemployed for so long. I enjoy it more now. I feel useful. I do a lot at work because I want to be useful. I think unemployed people if they want to work and when they do find a job, they work harder because they realise how long they've been unemployed and, you know, they want to be useful. *(Fiona, Manchester)*

It is, because then you don't get bored and you have something to do during the day and go out every morning and the day's nearly gone. So I think it's really good to have a job . . . it makes you feel wanted, makes you feel that you can do a job. *(Mary, Southampton)*

The difference between men and women in this regard is only one of degree, however, in that a clear majority of men echo women's views about the importance of work in their lives. On all of these issues between 60 and 70 per cent of the men in our study responded affirmatively. However, one small group, representing approximately 15 per cent of all the men, consistently downplayed the importance of employment. The majority of these men lived in the North, and although their experiences in the labour market did not distinguish them from the others in any significant respect, their views on the importance — or lack of importance — of employment set them apart:

It's not important to me, no . . . We're always told that you should be working because of this or you should be working because of that — but you're never told when you're unemployed, nobody ever says to you, 'that's alright, you're not working because . . . ' It's never seemed all that important to me, having a job. It's not something you can explain. It's not all important to me. The only thing that people got to work for is to get money. I've got enough money as I am, so it doesn't bother me. *(Nick, Sheffield)*

I don't know. I suppose if they've got enough to do in their leisure time and they've got enough money to do it, I don't see why they should really work. *Interviewer: Is it important for you to have a job?* I think you'd be better asking me that in a few years' time, really. *(Patrick, Sheffield)*

No, not anymore. I don't think it'd be too important now that I should have a job. I think I've got used to not having one. *(John, Sheffield)*

For the majority, however, having a job was important.

Perhaps the best indicator of the importance of employment in the lives of the young people in the study was their recognition of the difference that having a job made to their moods, to the way they felt about themselves and, of course, to their pocket-books:

Yeah — a lot happier. For the reason, more money and I can go out now at weekends, meet people. But out of work you can't do that. *(Ceri, Manchester)*

In a job you feel a lot better about yourself . . . I feel as though I've actually achieved something at the end of it . . . changed my life, finding all these things to do. *(Edward, London)*

A bit happier. I'm a very moody person anyway and actually I'm not so moody these days. I've sort of, you know — I feel grown up now, feel a bit more grown up and feel as if I've got something there, something behind me, so I'm happier. *(Fiona, Manchester)*

Oh yes. Well, when I first got it I was over the moon. After a year you get — well, I'm still glad I've got a job. I wouldn't do without this job for anything. *(Donald, Southampton)*

The four young people quoted above were all in employment when interviewed. However, even those young people who could only think back in time to the days when they had been employed remarked upon the difference having a job made, whether or not that job was sometimes boring or (usually) poorly-paid:

Bored, yes. I mean when I was working there was days when I — well, I hated going into work, you know, because the job was boring . You know, like one night — oh well, you think: 'Oh God, the same old faces — the same old job'. Every job gets boring after a while, but it's better to be bored in work than bored out of work. *Interviewer: Would you say you enjoyed life more when you were working?* Yes, you do. Like I said, it gives you that sense of independence. I mean if I saw anything in the shops I knew I could go out and buy it. Now [that I'm unemployed] I just look at things and think: 'In about three weeks I might be able to afford that if I go steady'. *(Kate, Sheffield)*

I feel a lot happier within meself like, when I'm working. When you get the pay packet, you've got something to show for it, like. *Interviewer: Did the money from working make a difference?* No, not really, 'cos jobs what I've had's been low paid anyway, so more or less sort of always been on the breadline . . . Now, I'm — well, how can I put it — me temper is more short like, you know? (Doug, Sheffield)

Three-quarters of the young men and women who had been in employment at some time prior to the interviews reported positive changes in their moods when in work, with no differences between men and women or by geographical area. Only 6 men and one woman felt they were happier out of work than in; only 2 men felt unable to comment by virtue of never yet having had jobs which they enjoyed. And this is despite the fact that one-quarter of both men and women reported having been bored in previous jobs, and despite one-quarter of the men reporting that the money they earned in work was not sufficient to make much difference to their lives.

From one perspective, it is not particularly surprising that these young people place such importance upon having jobs, nor that they feel happier within themselves when in work. It has been suggested however, that for some young people exchanging bad jobs for good unemployment is very much a preferred option. As Roberts notes: 'describing some of the jobs offered to unqualified school-leavers as unskilled fails to convey their depressing characters' (1982:11). Low pay, poor working conditions, no opportunity for training, and repetitive, boring work-tasks are too often the main characteristics of the jobs available to young people in the lower segments of the labour market. The normal pattern of frequent job-changing found among less well-qualified school-leavers and young people during their first years in the labour market thus becomes understandable, as does the preference of unemployment to a bad job. However, the young people of this study were well beyond their first years in the labour market, in terms of age if not in work experience. When interviewed, the youngest respondents were aged 20 and the oldest, 26-27. And it is this fact — the fact of growing up both chronologically and socially — which might well account for the importance they so clearly placed on having jobs. The words of the following young man from Manchester illustrate the change in perspective which growing up can bring:

Interviewer: Is it important to you to have a job? I don't know. Being unemployed in the summer's great, it's really good. I'd say yes definitely over the winter months, but I'm not bothered in the summer. But in the future, you've got to look for work, haven't you? That's your life, isn't it? If you want a family, you've got to work. When you're young, up to 20, work doesn't matter as much because you don't care much about anything anyway. They say it's when you get between 21 and 25 that you start realising you need work. You just become more aware of the world and what it's like. *(Colin, Manchester)*

And when jobs are important, you simply keep looking.

Avoiding unemployment

The present study allows further measure to be taken of the importance assigned to having employment by the young unemployed. First, respondents were asked if they had ever taken a break from employment, either to escape from a bad job or just to have a rest. Only 5 young people had ever left a job just to take a rest — so small a proportion that it is hardly worth analysing. Jobs had been left for other reasons, however, including low pay, poor working conditions, and lack of training opportunities. Far more often, though, young people left jobs because they were made redundant. Secondly, respondents were asked if they would stay in a job they disliked, or one which was poorly-paid, simply to avoid being unemployed. This general question was followed up by reference to specific working conditions. And finally, respondents were asked if there were any jobs they positively would not do. The responses to this area of questioning confirm the high value these unemployed young men and women place on having jobs.

Analysis of the replies to the more general question about avoiding unemployment reveals clear differences between participants. However, because of the very small number of women living in the South included in the study (11), it is not clear whether these differences are a matter of gender, or if they can be accounted for by differing labour market conditions between the North and the South. In general, the women of this study were more likely (70 per cent) than the men (55 per cent) to say that they would stay in work simply to avoid unemployment. Disaggregation by geographical region, however, indicates that it is generally the men living in the South who would be willing to exchange paid work for the dole if they were unhappy in their jobs. Only just over one-third of men in the South would stay in a job regardless, in comparison with 70 per cent of the men in the North. Men in the North, then, adopt a similar stance to women in their willingness to continue in unsatisfactory work rather than re-enter unemployment:

> Some people, they get a job, if they don't like it, they leave. I think it's important that you stick to a job even if you don't like it . . . there's a lot of jobs that I wouldn't do but that I'd take, if you understand what I mean. With being on the dole, you've got to take anything. *(Bob, Manchester)*

> Not really. It'd depend if I liked the job or not. Not really, because I've been out of work and I know what it's like. But if the job was worth having, then I'd stick it. I would stick it . . . but no, not necessarily hang on to it just because I've been unemployed for quite a long time period. *(Leroy, London)*

> I think I'd think twice about it. I mean I'd give a job — if I didn't like a job — I'd give it a second chance rather than come out of work. *(Kate, Sheffield)*

> No, I wouldn't leave. I'd stay in a job until I got something else if I didn't like it. *(Stephanie, London)*

As noted above, the general question on avoiding unemployment was followed up by questioning about whether respondents would accept jobs with various different characteristics, including low pay, part-time hours, travel distance to work, shift work, night work, dirty work, and co-workers consisting predominantly of older people or people of the opposite sex. The last three of these working conditions and the distance to be travelled to work proved relatively unimportant to virtually all respondents. Men tended more often than women to object to part-time hours and low-paid work, while women were less inclined than men to undertake shift work or night work. In no instance, however, did more than one-quarter of respondents object to any one condition.

In some instances marital status was linked to differences in attitudes. For example, all married women would accept part-time work, while a small number of unmarried women would refuse. Married and unmarried men, on the other hand, were equally likely to refuse or accept part-time hours. Further, married men were more or less equally divided between accepting or refusing low-paid work, while unmarried men tended to say that they would refuse, or that acceptance would depend upon other conditions such as the nature of the job, prospects for job training, or travel distance to work. Few other differences were found between married and unmarried people.

However, among those respondents who would refuse certain types of work, some differences were identified between areas. Although the men in the North responded affirmatively more often than not to the general question about avoiding unemployment, they proved to be more particular about specific types of jobs than their Southern counterparts, with the single exception of low-paid work. And all men proved to be more particular than all women about specific working conditions, with the exception of night work and shift work. Phrased slightly differently, when asked if they would undertake specific jobs, say ones that involved part-time hours or low pay, men often said no, despite the fact that they had previously stated that they would stay in a job simply to avoid being unemployed. Women, on the other hand, tended to be more consistent in their responses:

> *Interviewer: Would you stay, just to avoid unemployment?* Yes, it would make me stick in a job *Interviewer: Would you take a job that's low paid?* Yes, because when I first started at (firm), they took me on at 16 hours so I was only earning £5 more than when I was signing on. But it was worth it, just to get out. *(Grace, Sheffield)*

> I think any job you get nowadays, you've got to stick with it. *Interviewer: Would you accept low pay?* No, I'd rather be unemployed if the job was paying less than unemployment benefit. It's not worth it. *(Martin, Sheffield)*

In addition to specific working conditions which respondents would prefer to avoid, the majority of both men and women were able to name specific jobs which they would be unwilling to undertake, with factory work, cleaning jobs, shop or office work, manual labour or building jobs each mentioned by about 10 per cent of respondents:

Interviewer: Are there any sort of jobs that you absolutely wouldn't do? Security guard, I suppose, standing still doing nothing all day, just watching something — your life's just ticking away and you're not doing something important. Wouldn't get any satisfaction out of just watching something. *(George, London)*

I don't know. I think that if you're prepared to do a job that is menial and tedious, like a cleaning job where you're getting only ten pounds a week more than you would if you were on the dole, then fair enough, do that. There are those jobs about, but I wouldn't. *(Marcia, Southampton)*

There's some work I wouldn't choose to take on . . . there's always nonsense like washing up and things like that for £50 a week — skivvying . . . And there's no point in digging ditches for £60 a week, because that's not going to get you anywhere; you're just labouring for an existence. I don't mind heavy work if I thought it was for an end, but not just to do it constantly for the sake of rubbing two pennies together. *(Michael, London)*

I wouldn't like to go back into shop work. I found it very — I don't know — I didn't like it, you know. I wasn't happy there and I think I wouldn't like to go back into that one ever again . . . it was very boring, in just having people all day and that's it — end of story. There's no enjoyment, no satisfaction out of it. You know, people don't think about buying food. They just do it. So, you know, they don't get any satisfaction and so you don't. *(Fiona, Manchester)*

Over half of the men and two-thirds of the women named one or more specific jobs which they would refuse. However, one in five women and almost one in three men reported that there were no jobs which they would not do. To their minds, anything would be better than remaining unemployed. Moreover, this apparent willingness to undertake whatever work they could find was often based upon concrete experience of rather unpleasant previous employment:

Interviewer: Would unemployment affect your decision to stay in work — would you stay in a job you didn't like? Yes. Because I did. I worked in a slipper factory — it was very very long hours — and I stuck that for six months and then the fire officer come in and shut the firm down. It was a mill that hadn't had any work done on it; the toilets used to let the rain in — and that was the end of that . . . it was very very low pay. It was very very poor. I worked eight hours a day, five days a week. I used to be there in the morning at eight o'clock, I used to have half an hour for my dinner, I used to be home at half past four, quarter to five I used to leave the factory. And I used to get £41. So of course that was very very poorly paid. And if I did any overtime, he used to give you 50 pence an hour for any overtime. But it was a job, so. *Interviewer: Are there any jobs you wouldn't do?* No, not really. *(Adam, Manchester)*

I am doing warehouse work. I don't know how to describe it — yes, that would be about it, a warehouse person. I have been there since September. I don't know if it's permanent. I'd been out of work for three or four years, and I needed a job now. So it was a question of getting whatever I could then. *Interviewer: Is there anything, any job, you wouldn't do?* I wouldn't know. *Interviewer: Like bad work, dirty work, badly paid?* That describes the job that I'm doing. There's not a lot of work that I wouldn't like to do. *(Steve, Southampton)*

In general, then, although having a job is very important to the majority of young people interviewed, and hence they continue their search, all but a minority maintain certain standards of acceptability about the work they would undertake. Like others in the labour market, unemployed young people want decent, well-paid jobs and not trashy, poorly-paid ones. This is not particularly remarkable, and has been found in other studies (Roberts, 1983; Willis, 1984); it is, however, a want that is rarely satisfied.

On the expectation that unemployed young men and women — who have yet to find continuous employment and who generally have yet to marry and start families — might prefer working hours which would allow them lots of spare time, respondents were asked if they could visualise any ideal combination of work and non-work. Further attestation to the importance of jobs to these young adults may be had from their responses to this question: just over half of the men and just under half of the women wanted full-time work, and could visualise no other combination of work and free time which would satisfy them:

A lot of my friends do that now. They work on those schemes where you work two and a half days a week and the rest of the time just go weight-lifting or football or whatever. They're quite enjoying it. I'd like a job, but if I was to work it would have to be full-time. I'd like to find a job that I enjoy and just do that for the rest of my life. You get better and better at it as time goes on. *(Colin, Manchester)*

No, because for what work you do, you are not getting paid enough and if it is a part-time job, you are doing bits-and-bobs and then someone else is coming in to finish your work off and I wouldn't like that, I like to do my own job. *(Janet, Sheffield)*

No, not really. Obviously it's going to be the money. It's nice having spare time, but if you're going to work, it's got to be full-time for the money. The same old thing, money: but that's what counts really. *(Leroy, London)*

About one in five of the men and 40 per cent of the women could think of some combination of work/non-work which they would be willing to do. Usually this involved some form of part-time working hours, often job-sharing, which was seen as a way of equalising the distribution of employment:

> My own views on it that jobs that need to be should be job shares. There should be a job-sharing scheme so that people who are unemployed can have a chance of work. You get spare time then in the afternoon or in the morning or whenever. And I think that would be fairer on a lot of people. With the present situation, yes. Because I think, if you take some jobs, where one fella does it five days a week, you can see he works one week on mornings, one week afternoons. It is fairer, because then everyone would get a little bit of a chance of earning some money and some people wouldn't get depressed. I'd like to do that, I think. But, of course, you don't see many jobs like that advertised. *(Adam, Manchester)*

> I've heard about sharing jobs and I think that's a good idea. We know people who've got two jobs. A lady we know has two jobs and two daughters who are unemployed. She hardly has any time to sit down and unwind. Her two daughters are at home all day and do nothing. I don't think you should have more than one job. It's like having three cars, you can only drive one at a time. *(Irene, Southampton)*

Having a job, then, was important to these young men and women, and because of its importance, full-time work was valued above extra spare time. Neither the experience of bad jobs nor years of unemployment had succeeded in diminishing the commitment of most of these young people to finding a place in the labour market. They might be young, they might not be heading for careers, but they did want work. But getting a job — whether full or part-time — is not as simple as wanting one. And so, in the absence of proper jobs, some young people spend their time on government schemes while others work casually in the informal labour market. The rest just wait.

Schemes
Slightly less than half of both men and women in the present study had participated in a government scheme of some type prior to inclusion in the initial 1984 survey, primarily the Youth Opportunities Scheme (YOPS) but also the TOPS courses. In addition, the Community Pro-

gramme (CP) had provided the chance for paid work. Only a small number of the younger men and women had participated in the Youth Training Scheme (YTS), although many more believed that YTS was in fact one of the schemes they undertook. Confusion over the naming of schemes is quite widespread, as is lack of differentiation between paid work through government schemes and non-scheme paid work. And for some of the young unemployed, the confusion extends to evaluation of the schemes themselves:

Well, there's these schemes and that, but I don't know whether they're a good thing or what. They're good in a way, but they're not in another sense. Because (firm) which is a department store or (firm) or somewhere, they're able to take people on these schemes, pay them dirt cheap, they don't have to pay them, and they say you're getting experience — it's stopping them employing someone else . . . They might be able to have ten people on this scheme, but they probably can't afford to employ ten people if them people weren't there on schemes, and they might need them ten people. Then that business would probably go down if they had to pay [full wages]. It comes a bit jumbled. *(Liz, Sheffield)*

I'd like to say get rid of these schemes because, surely that would create some more jobs; but then again, I can't say that because it was through one of them schemes that I got a job when I left school. . . . (firm) used to average about — I don't know if it was nine YTS kids — and there was no chance of a job for them. Yes, that shop needed those nine girls. But they knew the minute they were gone, they could get another nine. And they really did need those nine girls. Or perhaps not nine, but they may have needed, say, six. Whereas they didn't have to pay six wages if they got nine YTS instead. *Interviewer: Do you think that if schemes were scrapped there would be more jobs?* There'd be a few more, but obviously not much more, because people take YTS even if they don't need them. Then again, that's a good way in a sense because you are creating a few jobs, but then again, in the other sense, kids are coming straight out of school on the dole and they're just — that's it — nothing. *(Kate, Sheffield)*

Participation in schemes was not directly addressed in the interviews. Nevertheless, many young people initiated discussions of their experiences. In the main, these were unfavourable, with references made to racial discrimination, poor working conditions, and failure to provide the amount and type of training promised. However, the most common complaint was that jobs failed to follow their participation in the schemes. The following young men speak for others in the study:

31

I disapprove of all Youth Opportunities Schemes — all schemes. I think they're a load of rubbish. Further education is more important to someone of that age group [16] than any scheme . . . I mean, you'll get a certain percentage that say they were fantastic and we've all got jobs from them, but the majority are not getting anywhere. Because even if you do get a year — a year and a half's training in something like turning, engineering — I mean, there's still no job. And you haven't even got proper qualifications anyway. *(Philip, Sheffield)*

Well, you go on a scheme which lasts either six month or 12 month and after that you're back on dole. I've been on YTS schemes and that different schemes, so I don't know how many schemes I've been on. I've been on about four schemes [during three years' unemployment] . . . I get angry because I've never had a proper job . . . instead of putting money into schemes for 12 months, they should start to create some proper jobs. *(Bob, Manchester)*

One-third of the 55 young men and women who had participated in government schemes other than the Community Programme spoke critically of such schemes, and generally did so spontaneously rather than in response to questions from the interviewers. Favourable opinions of government-created schemes were held only by the smallest minority. From the majority, came remarks like the following:

Why work for £25 a week when — there's a job there, why don't they pay full money? (Daniel, Sheffield)

I think they should scrap the Youth Training Scheme and start getting proper jobs instead of spending all that money on things that are not going to last — because teenagers today, they're your future Prime Ministers and MPs, doctors, nurses, whatever. *(Helen, Manchester)*

I think they should set up more places for unemployed people where they can train. I don't mean like YTS and things 'cos a lot of people are on YTS, it's like slave labour, isn't it? You're doing work for nothing and you've got to go for two years now. *(Sue, Manchester)*

The views of these young people from the North are shared by their counterparts in the South. However, it is important to stress the selectivity of the views presented above. The young people of this study are generally young people for whom participation in schemes such as YOP or YTS had not been successful, in the sense that secure employment had failed to follow such participation. It is likely that, had they been successful in gaining employment after involvement in special employment measures, not only would they not have been included in the present research, their views about government schemes would probably have been markedly different.

Some unemployed young men and women have of course gained from government job schemes or training schemes. These young people were in the minority among those we spoke to, but they are part of the young unemployed nonetheless. Among these few, the new two-year Youth Training Scheme tends to be viewed with feelings approaching envy, as they wish such opportunities had existed for them on leaving school. Other young people favour participation in schemes quite strongly:

> Youngsters, school-leavers, have a bit more of a chance because of the Youth Training Scheme and things — they can take you on at 16 and they can take you on and pay you lower wages and everything. *(Ken, London)*

> I'd just say keep looking for work basically. Don't get lazy. I'd say they should go round to a few places and see if they have any vacancies. I think I'd say go on a course, and learn something — TOPS, YOPS — I think it's worth a go. *(Stephanie, London)*

> *Interviewer: Do you think it's worthwhile going on a scheme?* Yes, I definitely think it's worth it. It gives you experience, gives you something to do for a year or maybe two years, and while you are working you've actually got a better chance of getting a job — that's what most people find. *(Ben, Sheffield)*

Government schemes, whether for training or work experience, are official ways of occupying time usefully for people without proper paid employment. If lucky, a young person on such a scheme will learn a new skill or find a permanent job. If unlucky, well, there is always another scheme to try. Some of the young unemployed, however, look elsewhere for ways of filling their days and, with luck, earning extra money. Casual work can sometimes be one of these ways.

Casual work
Previous research has suggested that workers who lose out in the formal economy, through unemployment for example, will compensate by shifting to the informal economy and undertaking work on a casual basis (Rose, 1983; Pahl, 1984). However, as Roberts *et al.* (1984) point out, under present economic conditions there is considerable competition for informal work, and young people tend to lose out in the search for casual jobs. Only a minority ever succeed in adding to their income in this way. It was clear from our interviews that over two-thirds had never enjoyed opportunities for casual working, or had done so only rarely. Marked differences exist between North and South, reflecting differing labour

market conditions; men in the South are the most likely to work casually, women in the North the least likely.   Altogether, 28 men and 12 women had worked at casual jobs on more than one occasion, with only 6 men (5 from the South) and one woman doing so frequently. Among the study group, then, casual work undertaken on a *regular basis* is quite rare. For the majority of both men and women, casual work either forms no part of their lives at all, or figures only intermittently.

There are two main reasons for the lack of casual working among the young unemployed of this study: no available jobs and too much risk. About half of the men and women said that they did not undertake informal work because either there was none available or they did not know where to find the work which did exist. The slight differences between men and women in this regard are over-shadowed by differences between areas, with young people in the North considerably more likely than those in the South to cite non-availablity of work as their primary reason for not working casually. Moreover, a further one-quarter of both men and women felt that the risks involved in working casually without informing the benefit office, and thus losing part or all of their dole money, far outweighed any advantages which might be gained. Neither differences between men and women nor between North and South separate these young people in wishing to avoid risk:

Interviewer: Have you ever done any casual jobs? No . . . Mainly because I'm frightened that they'll find out — I don't want to be left with no money at all. *(Doug, Sheffield)*

Occasionally there was a bit of bar work. I used to get asked — 'Oh, would you like to do the bar at the dance club down the road?' No, none of us ever did. It wasn't worth the hassle. 'Cos we always used to think: 'Are we the ones that got found out?' I never did . . . it just wasn't worth the hassle. I know people that've done it and have got caught in the end and, you know, I wouldn't want to. *(Fiona, Manchester)*

Yes, I know. I couldn't do it. I don't know, I had an offer once and that was working on a building site and it was only picking up, shovelling cement all up together and I thought about it — 'can't give you an answer straight away. I'll think about it'. I thought to myself, if I get caught I'll lose my dole. I'll lose everything. I've got a wife and kids — is it worth it? Me and the wife had a long talk about it and then decided no. I don't know how long I was going to be out of work, but at the time we decided no because at the same time if we lost it, we'd have lost everything. You know what I mean, and then what would we have done? *(Baljit, Southampton)*

In addition to avoiding risk, the difficulties involved in coming on and off the dole entailed by taking up casual work legally were mentioned by respondents. If at all possible, hassle, especially with the authorities, is to be avoided:

> I haven't been able to [work casually]. The lady in the Jobcentre said it doesn't really pay. She'd only advise married women who don't claim unemployment benefit to do that. Sometimes it's only for a week, then you have to tell the benefit people that you've got a job for a week. And when it finishes, tell them you are unemployed again. It takes too long, it's all red tape. *(Irene, Southampton)*

Casual work, then, is not the experience of the majority of young people in the present study. As noted above, however, a number of men and women had had at least some experience of casual work, if only on one or two occasions. In the North, such work is as likely to be done for relatives and friends as for strangers, while in the South, working for strangers is the norm. When asked, very few men or women reported that they told the authorities about their casual earnings, despite considerable fear of being found out:

> There's more work to do here [as opposed to Manchester] — building work and that kind of thing . . . I don't see it worth telling [but] it was a constant worry actually. You see people stood at the corner of the street and wonder if they were from the DHSS . . . If they made it a better situation to get a part-time job, I wouldn't do any casual work. *(Charley, London)*

> Yes, it's always in the back of your mind that there could be somebody watching you, or you might get nosey neighbours, like we've got, that know you've been out even before you know. *(Martin, Sheffield)*

For some, though, worry was absent. The system had not been fair to them: why should they be fair to it?:

> *Interviewer: Did it frighten you that you might get found out?* No, not really. I think I'm like everybody else in them situations — if you're like, you get a bit hard done to, and you been on the dole for a long time. I mean, you're not going to go and report the first bit of money you get in something like a year, and get it took away — be a fool to yourself, I think. *(Philip, Sheffield)*

> Tell the DHSS? Why should I tell them? I mean, really — they're only going to, like, say this, that and the other. I'm just trying to help meself out really. I mean, everyone does it — if they find out, they find out. I keep myself to myself really; I don't worry about that at all. *(Leroy, London)*

Interviewer: Did you ever tell the DHSS? Well, I didn't see the point really, because what I was getting off them wasn't enough to live on, so if I would have told them about this money I'd earned, maybe they would have cut my benefit even more. That's how I thought about it. I've got to think of meself first, so I thought best not to. *(Aziz, Manchester)*

The money earned by these young men and women rarely amounts to much: an extra £5 or £15 a week when work is available, and long stretches between these weeks when little or no work can be found. One young man, however, was fully committed to work in the informal — and illegal — sector. Daniel lives in the North. He had been out of work six times since leaving school in 1975 without qualifications — representing more than five years' unemployment. His jobs had mainly been on building sites although he once had dreams of being a fireman or an airline pilot. He still hoped to find success as a musician. In the meantime, he had spent the last two and a half years fly-posting notices of future rock concerts, a job he bought from its previous holder. Initially, Daniel continued to sign on for benefits, but his first trip to court put an end to this:

Cause [I] got nicked last June. I went to court and the guy I were working with, like he were working self-employed all by himself, and I just said I were doing it for a favour. And then I thought if I get caught again some bloke would sort it out, so I stopped [signing on]. He carried on then, but then he moved on. So he said: 'Well, business is yours if you want to buy it off me'. So I took the plunge . . . I can see what'll happen eventually is like I'll just keep on going on and on to court, like, fines will get more and more and more until eventually they say: 'Right, next time you do it — jail' . . . It is illegal but the police take a lenient view on it and things like — it's only 1 in 50 what will book you. And you have to go to court and things, like on Wednesday, got fined £20. The company pays, so there's no problem . . . it's not exactly boring; you're looking for a police car all the time; you haven't got time to get bored — you're on the go all the time . . . Mum, I reckon now she's proud of me, because of this job. She doesn't know exactly what I'm doing, just — you know . . . It'll end sometime in the future, in the next ten years.

The extent of criminal work in the economy is not known, as such work is not registered in official statistics. No other young people interviewed for this study reported engaging in activities similar to Daniel's enterprise. It is possible that Daniel is not alone, and that other young people included here participate in illegal work — shoplifting, selling drugs, receiving stolen goods. There were, however, few indications of this in interviews; few shared Daniel's sense of danger or his rather casual approach to the likelihood of an eventual jail sentence. Although perhaps that was only because they had not had Daniel's opportunities.

The obvious advantage of undertaking casual work is the money it brings, money which can supplement a usually insufficient dole. The obvious disadvantage is getting caught, and losing access to benefits. And for all but a few of the young men and women interviewed, the disadvantages of casual work — combined with its scarcity — meant that little work in the informal sector was undertaken. It may well be, of course, that more of the young unemployed work casually on a regular basis than the few who reported doing so in interviews. After all, such work is illegal, if one is claiming benefits. However, as Pahl's research on the Isle of Sheppey suggests, it is rarely those without work in the formal economy who work in the informal sector — if only because they lack the necessary material and equipment (Pahl, 1984). Given this fact and the competition for any kind of work at all in areas of high unemployment, it is unlikely that the results of this study are misleading regarding the small part played by casual work in the lives of most of these young people.

Voluntary work

Only a very small number of men and women had undertaken work in the voluntary sector: 8 men and 5 women, although more than twice this number had considered unpaid work. For a few, the vagaries of signing on for benefits stopped them from offering their services to voluntary organisations:

> Yes, I considered it when I was first unemployed, but they said they'd stop me benefit and I couldn't afford to, you know, stop me benefit. They said at the beginning that if I did over a certain amount of voluntary then they'd stop so much out of me money. It was because if I wasn't — if I was doing voluntary work I wasn't eligible for work. *(Eileen, Manchester)*

A much more frequent explanation for not undertaking voluntary work, however, is the apparent reluctance of voluntary organisations to hire these unemployed young people:

> I went to the Voluntary Work Bureau and put my name down and told them what sorts of things I wanted to do, and they said 'We've got lots of jobs like that'. They never wrote to me, they never got in touch with me. I had to ring them up and said perhaps they had lost my form and they said they would get in touch again and that they had written [to her previous employer]. But I never heard from them again. *(Marcia, Southampton)*

I've considered it. But, whenever I've been seen about it, its always been, 'Oh, well, come again in a couple of days or do this or do that'. So it's disinterested me in the fact that whenever I've gone, it's always, 'Oh well, we're a bit busy at the moment, come back and see us in a couple of days' time'. So, of course, that disheartens you, so you think, 'Oh well, they mustn't want any help, that's the end of it'. *(Adam, Manchester)*

It is hard enough when no-one wants to pay you to work, but when you are unable even to give your labour away, life can get very discouraging. In the main, however, voluntary work was not viewed as an option by these young people. As three young men noted: if a job is worth doing, it's worth being paid for. It is not voluntary work that is wanted: it's jobs.

Notes

1. The differing family and childcare responsibilities of men and women in our society are reflected in the benefit system and hence by the drop-out rate of women from registered unemployment. Sample selection for the 1984 survey was based upon registration for benefit, thus when selected in February 1984 all married women in the survey were registered as unemployed. By the time of the interviews in May/June 1984, however, only 42 per cent of married women remained as registered unemployed. By October 1985 when the postal questionnaire follow-up was conducted, only 21 per cent of married women remained in registered unemployment. Further, Labour Force Survey estimates for 1985 suggest that as many as one million married women are not registered as unemployed but are seeking work (Meade-King, 1986). See Chapter 4 of this study for further discussion of this issue.

2. See, for example, the work of Ashton and Field (1976) who write:

. . . prolonged unemployment is likely to pose less of a problem for the young women. In the first place . . . work is not usually as important to them as it is for the young men. Secondly, the young woman can contribute to the effective running of the household through taking over household tasks of various kinds which in some cases may even free their mothers for work. (1976:104)

3 QUALIFICATIONS AND TRAINING

Introduction

In keeping with the overall aim of making sense of the world confronting the unemployed young men and women in this study, the objective of this chapter is to document their views about the relationship between education and their experiences in the labour market, including the possibility of further training. This will be done, first, by outlining what has become known through policy-oriented and academic research about the relationship between qualifications and employment; and, second, by establishing the beliefs of the young unemployed about this same relationship. An attempt will then be made to relate the beliefs of the young unemployed to their actions. The chapter includes a discussion of the highly-qualified young unemployed, and concludes with a brief look at unemployed young men and women from middle-class family origins.

The unemployed young men and women of this research are in general as well — or as poorly — qualified as their employed counterparts in the labour market. An important finding of the 1984 survey of the young unemployed from which respondents were drawn demonstrates that, when position in the occupational strata is taken into account, it seems *improbable that the young long-term unemployed are substantially inferior in qualification levels to other young people working in the lower half of the job market.* It would therefore be misleading to characterise the young unemployed as forming a large pool of unqualified labour. Although the unqualified are particularly likely to be in long-term unemployment, they form less than half of the total. Moreover, the tendency for the unqualified to stay longer on average in unemployment is more or less offset in aggregate by the progressively increasing inflow of qualified young people into unemployment. Few differences in qualification levels exist between respondents to the 1984 survey and the young men and women included here. Table 3.1 below indicates the qualifications obtained by the young unemployed of both studies.

Table 3.1 Educational qualifications of the young unemployed

	column percentages			
	1984 Survey (unweighted)		Present Study	
	Men	Women	Men	Women
CSE below grade 1 only	20	22	27	21
O-level/SCE O	23	30	16	33
A-level/SCE H	7	7	5	5
None	49	40	52	40
Base	*776*	*334*	*76*	*43*

As shown, slightly more of the young men included in the present re-port obtained CSEs below grade 1 and slightly fewer obtained O-level or higher qualifications, while the proportion of men failing to obtain any qualifications at all was roughly equal. Moreover, there are no differences between the men by year of entry into the labour market. However, when this factor is taken into consideration for women, differences in levels of non-qualification are found between the two groups. Just over half of the young women in the present report who entered the work-force in 1975-79 did so without qualifications, in comparison with only 39 per cent in the full national survey, while in the later years 1980-83, less than one-third of the women in the present report entered the labour force unquali-fied in contrast to almost 40 per cent of the national sample. Only slight differences in levels of qualification obtained exist between the women in the two groups with respect to CSEs, O- and A-levels. It is not clear why there are these few differences in non-qualification between the women of the full national sample and those included in the present study, but given the preponderance of women from the North it is possible that they can be accounted for by variations in qualification by geographical area. All that is important here is that, among the women at least, some few differences exist which should be borne in mind throughout the follow-ing analyses.

Qualifications and employment
Previous research focusing on young people in the labour market has established a number of relationships between qualifications and employ-ment chances. First, qualifications control the points of entry of young

people into the labour market, with differences in qualification levels between broad occupational strata being considerably greater than differences in qualification between employed and unemployed young people in the lower segments of the labour market[1]. Secondly, repeated studies have shown that lack of qualifications tends to be associated with relatively less successful experiences of the labour market, and in particular, with unemployment[2]. Thirdly, among young people competing for jobs in the lower occupational strata, slight superiority in qualifications can nonetheless offer some advantage in avoiding very long durations of unemployment[3]. And fourthly, the more or less simultaneous increase in the rate of qualification among school-leavers and in the rate of youth unemployment has resulted in wholly unqualified 16-19 year olds coming to represent a diminishing proportion of all 16-19 year olds in unemployment, or, in other words, has resulted in an increased presence of qualified school-leavers among the unemployed[4].

To sum up these findings then: failure to acquire qualifications increases the likelihood of young people entering into competition for jobs in the lower occupational strata and, hence, increases their likelihood of unemployment. At the same time, however, the surplus of qualified school-leavers competing for jobs in the lower occupational strata means that the acquisition of qualifications may well not prevent any individual school-leaver from entering unemployment. DES Statistics of Education for 1975-81 clarify these points[5]. In 1975, only 15 per cent of *all unqualified 16-19 year olds* were in unemployment, but by 1981 more than 60 per cent of the unqualified in this age group were unemployed: a striking summary of the disadvantageous position in the labour market confronting the non-qualified. Over these years, however, unqualified 16-19 year olds in unemployment represented a progressively smaller proportion of all unemployed in this age group, decreasing from just under half in 1975 to less than one-third in 1981. Put the other way, this trend means that *qualified* school-leavers came to represent approximately two-thirds of all school-leavers in unemployment by 1981. If this is what is known to researchers, what then is known to the young unemployed themselves, and with what consequences for their actions?

Staying on

'I mean 16 is 16, you done your term and that's it really'.

The words of this young Londoner of West Indian origin speak for many others: 16 is perceived by a great number of young people and parents alike as the normal age to leave school for work, despite the fact that under present economic conditions it is often this decision which presages entry into unemployment. At the very least, early school-leaving

41

closes the possibility of acquiring qualifications beyond the minimum level and thus restricts the occupational strata within which young people can compete for jobs. Findings from the Oxford Social Mobility study demonstrated that class differentials in the acquisition of O-level and A-level qualifications could be almost wholly explained, for males at least, by the greater propensity of boys from professional and white-collar families to stay on in school beyond the age of 16. The O- and A-level examination results of the small proportion of working-class boys staying on beyond the minimum school-leaving age showed striking similarity to those of their classmates from middle and professional class families (Halsey, Heath and Ridge, 1980).

In the present study, more than 70 per cent of the women and almost 85 per cent of the men left school at or before the age of 16, with approximately half of each sex doing so without qualifications and a further 30 per cent having obtained only CSEs below grade 1. The majority of the young unemployed in the present study were, then, early school-leavers with either minimal or no qualifications. However, children from working-class homes have tended to leave school early and with poor examination results for many decades and have, in the past, found employment despite their lack of qualifications. What seems to have happened to the generation of working-class children leaving school between 1975 and 1983 is that the rules of the game have changed, leaving them not only poorly qualified or unqualified but unemployed as well. This seems to be especially true for the young men and women who left school between 1975 and 1979, many of whom were initially successful in the labour market only to find themselves unemployed in later years, as the words of these young people illustrate:

> . . . it was straight for work for me. . .there was no problem at the time, jobs were just — you could get a job near enough t'where you wanted them times. I suppose they [his parents] thought it was better for me working, rather than staying on. *(Sammy, Manchester, left school 1979)*

> Well, they encouraged me but I didn't do very well. It was just a waste of time going to school. . .at that time you could just walk into jobs. *(Karen, Manchester, left school 1976)*

> I did have a job to go to anyway, I knew me results wouldn't be good enough to be able to stop on, so I was looking for a job and actually got one a couple of months before I had to leave. . .I think it was a lot easier then — there were more jobs available at that time, so I don't think there was any real problem. *(Patrick, Sheffield, left school 1977)*

> . . . I didn't really enjoy school so I don't think they wanted to push me into staying on because they knew I didn't enjoy it very much. . . when

I left school there wasn't so much the problem of unemployment as there is now, no. I think jobs were easier to come by so I don't think they were so worried then as if I'd left now and they'd be much more worried but I don't think they were so then. *(Ken, London, left school 1979)*

Most of the young unemployed leaving school during 1975-79 expected to find employment. Their confidence is clearly expressed in the above quotations. Moreover, the majority did in fact find work, with only about one in five failing to do so in comparison with nearly three-quarters of those leaving school between 1980 and 1983. However, as youth unemployment continued to increase, the expectations of school-leavers changed, and unemployment became the anticipated destination of young people entering the labour market during 1980-83:

Interviewer: Did you expect to find a job when you left school? Well, not immediately. I thought it would take a bit of time before I actually found one. I thought it would be quite a while, but I didn't realise quite how long it would be. . .they [her parents] knew it was going to be hard, but I knew it was going to be hard as well. *(Jean, Sheffield, left school 1982)*

No, I already knew there was, what, three million unemployed when I left. . . *(Steve, Southampton, left school 1980)*

No, I knew what the job situation were like. . . *(Nick, Sheffield, left school 1982)*

Often the decision to leave school for work was taken in the light of the experiences of parents or older siblings in the labour market, experiences which had taken place under less harsh economic conditions:

No, they [his parents] weren't bothered. They said it's not worth it. They said just do what, you know, what you want. They said it's not really worth getting O-levels — that don't get you nowhere. [But I] don't know if they realised how hard it was to get a job: 'go on, go out and get a job'. It's not as easy as that. *(Donald, Southampton, left school 1982)*

Me mum did, she said 'Why don't you stay on?' And I said, 'No, I want to leave school and get a job'. They said to me afterwards — they tried to talk me into it . . . then they said, 'Well, you know, it's up to you and if you want to make that decision, it's yours. Don't come back to us when you can't find a job and say, Oh, it's not fair'. They told me that when I left school. They said you might not be able to find one. . .[but] when me brother left school, he found a job straight away, you see. I did at first but then it didn't last; then I found another one and that didn't last. *(Jenny, Sheffield, left school 1981)*

The majority of young people in this study reported that the decision to leave school at the age of 16 was almost entirely their own. A few parents apparently tried to convince their children to stay on but gave way in the face of opposition from sons and daughters. Many of the young people, of course, had no option but to leave school for work, as truancy or lack of ability had meant that they had taken no examinations. It has sometimes been suggested that class differentials in school-leaving age, and the disproportionate tendency for children from working-class homes to leave at the earliest possible opportunity, are the result of differing levels of middle- and working-class parental interest in the education of their children[6]. In this study, however, only a minority of young men and women reported that their parents were 'not bothered' about their school performance; rather, more than 70 per cent of those discussing this issue reported encouragement from their parents. Perhaps the explanation behind the early school-leaving of these young people lies not in any general lack of parental interest, but in out-of-date beliefs about the unimportance of school qualifications as a route to employment. Several young people reported their parents' lack of understanding about how much more difficult it has become to find jobs. This appears to stem from the parent's (usually but not always, the father's) own lifelong employment and success in the labour market with no formal qualifications prior to work-entry. Radical changes in the labour market between the generations have resulted in parents' beliefs being out of step with their childrens' experiences.

What we have seen above is the effect that passage of time and rising unemployment have had on the expectations of some young unemployed themselves about their job chances at the minimum school-leaving age. In general, the young men and women leaving school between 1975 and 1979 expected to find work despite failing to obtain school qualifications, while those leaving in 1980-83 tended to expect unemployment as their immediate destination, even with qualifications. Of course, not all the young people in this study can be categorised in this way. Some few of the school-leavers in 1975-79 expected, and entered, unemployment; some few leaving in 1980-83 expected, and found, employment. Over these years considerable flux existed both in the labour market and in the role qualifications play in avoiding unemployment, particularly in the occupational segments within which these young people are seeking work. In effect, the rules of the game changed after these youngsters began to play. And it would be only reasonable to assume wide variation in the amount of accurate information about these changes filtering through to those most directly concerned. The experiences of one young man from Manchester who left school in 1980 sum up the nature of these changes, and illustrate the consequences of time-lags in the dispersal of knowledge about the labour market:

Staying on? No, not for what I wanted, there was no need really. Qualifications you had to get was getting a job and then building it up and then you serve your apprenticeship or whatever. But for college, you can't. If you want to be a mechanic, like different sorts of mechanics, some are at this college, but mechanic on car, it's garage. You've got to work in a garage as their apprentice and then after three or four years, you get a qualification then. So it's not a college qualification, you know, it's not what you go to college for. . .[but] . . .the jobs that are going now are for qualified, like, mechanics, rather than somebody whose like learnt by experience. It's the qualification they want rather than what you know — like I, say I go for an interview in a garage and they say well, 'Where've you worked?' — 'I've worked in different garages' — 'What qualifications?' — 'Well, I haven't got any, I've just worked in the garages', and so you don't get the job. And really, that is only for a piece of paper. *(Martin, Manchester)*

Training
It is generally accepted that people stay on in school and obtain qualifications in order to improve their job prospects. From one perspective, the benefit of obtaining a qualification depends upon the difference that qualification makes to the individual's job prospects. The more people acquiring a given level of qualification, the more it makes sense — or becomes rational — for others to acquire the same qualification level. As we have just seen, however, the majority of young people in the present study did not stay on in school and either failed to acquire any qualifications or obtained only poor qualifications. Once out of school and into the labour market, however, the option of retraining for better, more marketable skills exists. Participants were asked if they had ever considered further training or education in order to improve their job prospects. Although a few had undertaken further training in the past (11 per cent) or were about to enter or were considering entering further education (10 per cent), the majority saw no benefit in doing so, often because of the visible presence of already qualified young people among the unemployed. This reaction lends support to the suggestion that once the number of qualified young people exceeds the number of job vacancies and the difference in job chances provided by qualification begins to decline, the incentive to acquire qualifications will also decline (Halsey, Heath and Ridge, 1980):

45

Yes, it was pretty easy then. Just ain't now. 'Cos now they're asking you for O levels, CSEs, and you're either too old or too young. *Interviewer: Do you think it's more necessary now to have qualifications of some sort, or training?* No, not really. 'Cos there's still youngsters that's been trained and highly qualified that still ain't got jobs. *(Dianne, Southampton)*

My father's a great one for the more education you've got the better job you'll get. Well, maybe 15 years ago that might have been the case, it's just not the case anymore. You hear so many people have got this and that and they can't get a job. They've spent all that time learning and they can't get a job. It's nice to be able to have a conversation with someone about anything and to know what you're talking about. I suppose to that extent it's good to have an education. *(Ian, London)*

No, because even when you go and do that — a couple of friends of mine did computer studies and things like that and when it came to the crunch, employers still prefer actual working experience. *(Helen, Manchester)*

Now I know. I thought I'd done enough by going to college. . . [but] you need experience of work. O levels aren't any good now. Everybody wants experience. The lady there [jobcentre] told me that a lot of university graduates haven't got jobs and the employers will skim the cream off and leave the rest, which isn't very nice. *(Irene, Southampton)*

Moreover, the acquisition of qualifications or further education without the subsequent acquisition of relevant employment can sometimes result in a downgrading of past achievement, not only in the eyes of others, but for the young unemployed themselves:

I used to say to my mother that I wish I'd never done my O levels and she'd say that they would help me sometime, which really they haven't. The two jobs I did get, I didn't need O levels for. When I was at the factory I had lunches with four other girls on the shift and they called us the 'brainboxes'. The lady who trained us on the machine didn't have half an O level, she'd been there all her life and was stuck there. A lot of girls came straight out of school to do it. They said we were stupid because we were on less pay than them. *(Irene, Southampton)*

I did two years of A-levels. . . I stopped on in the sixth form for a year, then I went to college for a year, and then it was two years before I found a job. . . with a Community Programme Scheme. . . there's no reasonable jobs on offer — it all seems to be experience needed, things like that. . . [now] I usually ask myself why didn't I leave school at 16, I could have gone on a YTS scheme and I might have got kept on. *(Jim, Manchester)*

These, then, are the two most common patterns found among those unemployed young men and women in the present study who reject the idea of further education: training or upgrading of qualifications which could perhaps significantly alter their chances in the labour market is held to be of little value either because of the highly visible presence of already-qualified young people in unemployment or because of the failure of their own qualifications to bring rewards in the labour market. In the eyes of many of the young people of this study, the qualifications obtained by friends or neighbours, by older siblings or by themselves, have failed to bring employment. This is what they see; what they believe to be true. Acting on this belief, they choose not to train. Rather than exhibiting *exceptional intransigence* in their attitudes towards the acquisition of new skills, as was suggested by an EEC survey of the young unemployed[7], these particular young people appear to be acting quite rationally.

Of course, other reasons prevent young unemployed people from seeking retraining, and they do not all share the belief noted above. Before examining the views of those who have undertaken further training or who simply believe in the efficacy of such training, some other factors which hinder re-training will be discussed. Paramount among them is money. Training itself can be expensive, and the ability to pay for such courses may mean disqualification from social security benefits:

I've been trying to get into computer studies; I've been finding out how just to get into it. There's a lot of people put you off, or that's what they seem to want to do. They keep telling me how hard the course is. . .I went to a seminar about two weeks ago, from (firm), and it was their aptitude test I did and they said I passed pretty well, like. Only they want something like £150 for me to do the first course. *Interviewer: Wouldn't you be able to get it paid for?* Well, at the seminar they said it's very difficult — they didn't really give very much advice on it. *(John, Sheffield)*

Yes, I thought about it [training] but the only thing is when you're unemployed and you are on the dole, you get used to the money and if you stop, you don't get any money. *(Joan, Manchester)*

I'm very good with cars, so I want to take a mechanic's course. I just can't afford it — it's £500, the course — you've got to pay for it, there's no government grant for it. I've checked up on that, and it's £500 and to get £500 with being unemployed, it's very, very hard. In fact, it's virtually impossible. *(Adam, Manchester)*

No, because when I went on the social they said that if I wanted to do a course, I'd have to pay for it myself and then — and they said that because — if I could pay for myself I shouldn't be claiming supplementary benefit. *(Eileen, Manchester)*

The accuracy of the information reported in the last quotation regarding ineligibility for social security benefits if one is able to pay for training courses might be questionable, but it is was the young woman from Manchester believed and, as a result, she felt unable to pursue training which might end her unemployment. Moreover, she was not alone in encountering a bureaucracy which hinders or prevents re-training. A young man from Sheffield wanted to pursue a computer training course in Leeds, despite the fact that it would mean leaving his wife and children alone during the week. He had previously decided against taking up a place on the Leeds course because it coincided with the birth of his youngest child and instead undertook a course in Sheffield. The Sheffield course failed to end his six years' unemployment, however, and bureaucratic regulations prohibited him from trying again in Leeds:

. . .I don't think I'll be able to get on that [TOPS course in Leeds] because . . .I went on another one in Sheffield and with doing that I think it's disqualified me for so many years. . .it's stupid really. I mean I could understand a year, but I think it's three years. What's the idea behind it? That you do one of their training courses and then spend three years looking for a job and if you can't, then try another one? *(Andrew, Sheffield)*

There is little reason to assume that this is an entirely unique experience. Bureaucratic regulations can prevent some unemployed people from obtaining training which would help them to acquire more stable footholds in the labour market, and this young man's experience has quite probably been shared by many others. Similarly, the technological inadequacy of the course offered to a respondent in Southampton which discouraged him from taking up the opportunity to retrain is doubtless to be found in other training opportunities. This young man was at first intrigued, but finally dissuaded from re-training:

. . .down at the Manpower Services — I've had a look at them but it's one of them — the Skill Centre is — I went round there and there was a course — thought it would be great, make something that looks quite nice. . . lathe turning and stuff like that all day in a workshop and it looked quite complicated as well. And they showed us this modern machine that's being brought in, so you got quite a lot — so I thought, I'm not going to train to be one of these, you get made redundant by this machine round the corner here, all computerised and that. So I thought I'll leave that one out. *(Billy, Southampton)*

It is, of course, quite likely that Billy was mistaken in not taking up the opportunity to train in that the unintended consequences of training — socialisation into work habits, demonstration to employers of both commitment and perseverance, occupation of time fruitfully — all outweigh the acquisition of skills which might someday become redundant. Clearly there is a need among some unemployed young people for better availability, and quality, of advice or guidance on training, if opportunities are not to be lost.

Another factor that hinders re-training by the young unemployed is age, which assumes importance in two ways. First, a few of the young men and women in this study felt that they were too old to pursue any further training, with remarks such as the following not uncommon:

Interviewer: Have you ever thought about getting more training or education which might give you new skills, or help you find work? Yes, I have but I'm 22 now, so I'm a bit too old for that. *(Terence, London)*

There's no courses at all, not for my age, because my age goes against me, with being nearly 23, it just goes against me now, I've checked. *(Adam, Manchester)*

In addition, however, is the view held by some of the young unemployed that their age tells against them by virtue of their being members of the wrong generation. It should be noted that this issue was not investigated systematically, rather it surfaced in some interviews. Nevertheless, there does seem to be a certain level of awareness among many of the young men and women of this study that theirs is the generation that has somehow been misled or has missed out:

It gets like a vicious circle. If you've never had a job, you haven't got experience, and then they won't take you unless you've got experience and this, that and the other. And then after a while, it gets so they want people just fresh out of school, so they can make them do the work for hardly paying them anything, or they want people who're just that bit older who've got several years experience behind them, and we're just caught in the middle. *(Jean, Sheffield)*

Both the young unemployed who left school without qualifications believing that they were not needed in order to find employment, and those who obtained qualifications only to discover that they were no longer effective in the search for work, seem to share this feeling. Many now see younger versions of themselves coming out of school and receiving much more adequate training through the YTS than that which was available to them. Others have been in unemployment for so long that they see any training as futile; as unlikely to lead to employment. The implications of these views are clear: coherent training programmes need to be created which will not only overcome any existent educational or skill deficiencies but also compensate for the growing disparities in attractiveness to employers between this generation of young people and the generation now leaving school. Furthermore, effective means must be found of communicating with the young people of the generation studied in the present research in order to change their beliefs about the efficacy — or lack of efficacy — of upgrading their qualifications and skills. Their own experiences in the labour market, and the experiences of their friends and neighbours which lead them to decide that training would only be 'a waste of time' must be countered in order to help them to become willing to risk investing in their own futures through training. Otherwise, this generation, or at least many members of this generation, will indeed be left behind, and the words of the following young man become true for many others:

> There is no prospect of having a settled job and I am getting fed-up with these schemes now. . . I am getting older. I feel as if I am rock-bottom. The school-leavers are getting further ahead [than me] on the two-year YTS. (*Vincent, Sheffield*)

When training is wanted

It was noted above that not all the young people interviewed for this report share the belief that training is futile or ineffective. Approximately 10 per cent had undertaken training or further education at some point after entering the labour market and a further 11 per cent were about to enter training or were thinking about doing so. It is perhaps significant that many of these young men and women left school during the years 1980-83 when knowledge about the need for qualifications was becoming more widespread. However, school-leavers from the years 1975-79 have also sought further training. One young woman who left school in 1978 was so convinced about the need for new skills that when her first attempt at upgrading failed to produce the desired results, she tried again:

> I did actually go on a course . . . to get secretarial skills and it didn't work out at first. It sort of petered out. I started the course and finished it and then I didn't do much with it and that's when I had a very long spell of unemployment. And then I went on a refresher course and found quite a few jobs after that. . . I don't think there was enough training, as such, on it [the first course]. It doesn't give you the experi-ence of work. It just gives you the experience of what to do — how to

type, etc. It doesn't actually give you, you know, a job situation where you could practise all that. . . .The second time I took more, you know, I did more things with the course and I got more things with it and I found that people needed those skills. . . it was audio, shorthand and word processing. In this day and age, you know, word processing is the one you need. (*Fiona, Manchester*)

After losing her original foothold in the labour market and enduring three spells of unemployment comprising just over four years, this respondent had been employed as a secretary for the previous twelve months. Other respondents also linked their desire for training or further educational qualifications directly to their unsuccessful experiences in the labour market. The following young woman hoped to end her three years' unemployment soon, and had continued to look for ways to do so despite lack of assistance from her local Job Centre:

. . . the only thing I've got is O-levels and I haven't done any training for a job, so I go for shops, factory work, anything. I'm taking short-hand and typing course at the moment, because all the jobs I've gone to they say: 'It's a pity you can't do typing' . . . I went to the Job Centre and they told me about audio typing. Actually, they haven't got many courses going down at the Job Centre. You can look them up in the computer and a lot of them were for Chartered Accountants. Obviously I haven't got any experience in chartered accountancy and then they said audio typing, so I wanted to do that but they stopped the course in March last year, so I couldn't do that. So I decided to take up night school. It takes two years to do the typing and shorthand. The teacher told me it takes five weeks to learn the basics and then you're half way there. So hopefully I may be able to get a job with that. Two weeks ago, somebody came in and said that someone who'd just fin-ished the course got a job teaching. (*Irene, Southampton*)

Or, as in the case of the young man below, the desire for training is linked to their fears of what the labour market might hold for them in the future:

Hopefully my job at the moment will last two or three years at the most. If I get a few more qualifications before I start looking again. Hopefully I will get my maths A level next year, or even take up one of these BTEC courses and see what happens. That is what I hope. I do expect to be out of work in the future with the kind of qualifications I have got now, but if I get some decent qualifications and a decent job, maybe I won't. But at the moment, I could be out of work tomorrow it is as simple as that. (*Steve, Southampton*)

It is unfortunately beyond the scope of the present study to determine why it is that some young people retain a sense of confidence in the efficacy of training and upgrading while other, apparently similar, young people come to believe the opposite. Given the importance to the young unemployed themselves of the consequences of these differing beliefs, it is clear that future research in this area is badly needed.

The highly-qualified

Nine participants in the present study stand apart from the others by virtue of their participation in higher education. Three young men and three young women had university or polytechnic degrees; and three other men were registered part-time students when interviewed. The experiences of these nine highlight some of the issues brought to the fore in this chapter.

Two of the three degree students entered their studies in response to their experiences in the labour market. The third, from Sheffield, had never been employed prior to starting a degree in English Studies despite the passage of seven years between leaving school and entering higher education. This young man, Pete, had a story to tell which differed sharply from the other students in that he was quite disturbed psychologically. Pete called himself neurotic, a recluse, and saw himself as *incorrigibly apathetic*. And although his troubles predated entry into the labour market, he suggested that unemployment could well have made matters worse:

> No, I mean, I felt bad before I left school. I used to sit in the corner, absolutely terrified of everyone. I don't know what came over me but — I was always pretty shy at school anyway, but something came over me when I was about 14 to 15, and I started avoiding everybody. Sitting in the corner. I didn't have any social skills at anything. I just avoided everybody. Pretty paranoid, really. And then I was thrown out. The teachers reported me to the headmaster: I was making everybody feel uneasy — 'he doesn't actually do anything — he just sits there'. So I was told to leave. So I don't think not having a job was the cause of my depression because I was feeling pretty bad before that. . . I think my problem was that I was left too much on me own, so I became more introspective, a bit morbid, and if I'd have had something to occupy myself, like a social situation, like a job, it might have done me a lot of good. That's the bad thing about being unemployed, if you tend to be a quiet type anyway, you could withdraw into yourself. I know a few people who've done that. I've got a friend in Liverpool who left school the same time as me. He's the only friend I ever had, and he's never had a job since, and he just stays in the house, except when

he signs on every two weeks, never goes out or has any friends or anybody, except me, to write to. It's pretty sad.

There are several others in this study who suffer pyschological distress in ways similar to Pete, and their experiences are related in a subsequent chapter. Pete differed from these others, though, in that he had sought education as a partial solution to his distress. Getting a job based upon the qualifications soon to be acquired appeared highly unlikely:

I mean, it was pretty bad before I started this degree. It gave me something to preoccupy myself, like studying, although I don't particularly enjoy studying, writing essays and whatnot. . . Most days I go into college, just sitting around. I don't attend seminars or anything. I don't attend most lectures. . . [But] at least I've got a bit of a social life at the moment, going to college, there's one or two people I can get along with, I play badminton once a week. But after college it's a great void, really. So I'm not really looking forward to the end of me degree. . .After college I can just see me getting bored, restless and nothing to do. It's a pretty empty life. . . I think it's only in recent years — in the last two or three — that I thought, Oh, maybe I could become a teacher. . . I must get something out of this course, English Studies, I could become a teacher, all that sort of thing, but I don't think I'd be a good teacher. So I'm not really sure. I'll just bide my time and see what happens. . .I don't think I've got the right temperament to be a teacher really. I just haven't got the initiative, I think. I think I'm probably so used to being out of work and not having a job. I think I've become incorrigibly apathetic, I'd have to change my whole attitude to life and myself. Maybe I will, I don't know. Probably a few years ago I was really determined to be a teacher, but since going to college I've realised that it's not for me. . .I can't really see me achieving anything as far as a career is concerned. I'm just basically apathetic. I can't help it. . . I can't really see meself doing anything really. Unless something crops up, I'll probably still be sat here.

The tragedy of Pete's story is his obvious intelligence. Had he left school with his two A-levels during a period of full employment, he would probably have found a job and, with that job, the possibility of mental stability. Perhaps he would still have found his way to college, but acting from confidence in his future rather than, as now, seeking company.

Two other young men were studying for degrees at the time of the interviews: both from Britain's ethnic minority population; one of Asian origin, the other West Indian. For both of them, the decision to enter higher education was influenced by their previous experiences of the labour market, though these experiences varied considerably, by virtue of differing years of entry into the work-force:

Yes, I have been unemployed before. . .at various times and various occasions for — I think the lengthiest period of time at any one time was about three to four months. . . At the time I left school — I'm trying to think over the years — to me it's a very long time ago, it's over ten years — but I don't think the unemployment situation, obviously, was as large as it is today. It was not as prominent, shall I say. Unemployment was there but it was not the focus of society that it is today, obviously because of the numbers. I was always interested in electrical type work, and I was fortunate in that I had an opportunity to actually work with somebody while at school and pick up a very basic understanding of electrical wiring through helping them and so on. So I decided that really that was basically what I wanted — I don't think the unemployment side of it really came into it that much, it was just the fact that I didn't intend to be unemployed whatsoever, I had no intention of signing on, or being unemployed for any lengthy period of time. I was determined to work and find suitable employment . . . I have faith in my abilities and the fact that I have studied for a lengthy period of time and have obtained quite a few qualifications in my particular field. (*Winston, London*)

Entering the labour market in 1976 had brought this young man of West Indian origin several, but short, periods of unemployment. His degree in electronics, combined with the work experience he had gained over the previous ten years, should ensure his occupational future. The experiences of the other young man, who left school in 1982, stand in marked contrast. Aziz lived in his parents' home with his wife and two sons. When interviewed, he was approximately half way through a three-year course leading to a degree in diagnostic radiography. He entered this course having failed entirely to find employment during the two-year period between school and college:

I realised that the qualifications I had at the time weren't enough to get the sort of job I wanted and so really, basically, the best thing was to carry on and get better qualifications and get a better job at the end of it. . .well, for a start, money, the money would be a lot better, better status, and I wanted to get into the sort of job where I could get, where there would be good promotion prospects rather than get stuck in a sort of dead end job with O-levels just required. . .I did understand the situation, you've got to to think of what it's like for everybody else, not just for yourself, you see. I knew there was people with degrees not employed and I only had O-levels and A-levels. (*Aziz, Manchester*)

Aziz believes that his failure to find employment prior to entering college was due, in part at least, to racism. He also believes that his education will bring him employment success in the future, although that future is unlikely to be spent in Britain:

> Whether people believe it or not, I think there is prejudice. Like, when you do go for a job, employers, their sort of way of thinking is: 'Why should we give the job to a coloured person when there's plenty of our own English people unemployed? So let's put them first before we give jobs to ethnic minorities'. That's how I think. . .I'm looking forward to qualification. I know once I've got that, NHS radiographers are sought after all over the world and once I've got that I know I've got a good qualification, I've got a definite chance, a good definite chance of getting a job *anywhere* in the world. . .what I was thinking of doing, getting a job abroad, because the wages here for a radiographer are £6000 on qualification. Whereas in Canada, places like that, you can get £12,000, better standard of living; and in places like Saudi Arabia, you can get £25,000 — tax-free! I can't really see meself living to the end of me life in this country — I just think it's really declining, you know, in our ways and moral ways — lots of ways, it's just going down the hole. I can't see it improving.

Although Britain will lose a skilled technician, Aziz is probably wise to go abroad. Overall, in 1985 unemployment rates for ethnic minorities were double those for whites, with a rate of 21 per cent among ethnic minorities in comparison with 11 per cent for whites; and among 16-24 year olds, the unemployment rate for ethnic minorities was 33 per cent in contrast to 16 per cent for whites (*Employment Gazette*, January 1987:27) Ethnic minorities represent approximately 4 per cent of the national total in unemployment. However, in the 1984 survey of the young unemployed, almost 9 per cent of male, and 8 per cent of female, respondents were classified as being of Asian, West Indian or African origin. In other words, young people of ethnic minority origin were over-represented in the 1984 survey of the young unemployed relative to the overall level of ethnic minority unemployment. Furthermore, young men of Asian origin *with qualifications* were shown in the 1984 survey to be differentially selected into unemployment in comparison with women or other ethnic groups, women of West Indian origin excepted. Just over 40 per cent of the Asian men in the national survey had O- or A-level qualifications in contrast to an approximate one-quarter to one-third of Asian women, West Indian men, and all white respondents. Over half of the women of West Indian origin had similar levels of qualification. Thus, although the absolute number of unemployed ethnic minority group members is small, the relative chances of young Blacks or Asians being selected into unemployment are high — even when they are well qualified. The presence among the six graduates in the present research of a further two men of ethnic minority origin who had still to find their first jobs illustrates just how likely unemployment can be as a destination for young Blacks and Asians.

Hasan was 26 years old, married, and, although a qualified electronic engineer, had been unemployed since leaving university three years ago:

> Well, naturally, I was looking for a job in electronic engineering. It was a job in general, rather than a specialised subject, maybe in communications, computers, or what have you. . .No, I've never had a job. . . yes, I was very surprised initially but then I realised that there were plenty of people in the same situation that I was, so after that, well, you don't really know which way to react, to be honest.... About two months ago, I enquired about something [training], a similar scheme which was radio and television, a course on radio and television. But unfortunately I couldn't get on that because I'm over-qualified, you see. . .At the moment I don't think I would draw the line anywhere, as long as it was a worthwhile job. (*Hasan, Manchester*)

Tony, a young man of West Indian origin, was also looking for work in the electronics field having finished a university degree in Physics one year prior to being interviewed. Tony went on to higher education because he was told that was the way to get a good job. But as he had failed to do so, he too — like Aziz — was thinking of looking overseas for better opportunities:

> *Interviewer: Why did you decide to go on to university?* Why? I just thought it would be a good idea at the time; the teachers said: 'You must go to University because you'll get a good job afterwards and so on', and that's it, I just thought it would be a good idea, I mean, why not? . . .Yeah, [I worry] a bit, yeah. Because I think that I might be unemployed for a long time if I don't get a job soon. Because the longer you're unemployed, the less employers want you and things like that. . . I'm fairly optimistic now, but I don't know if I will be later on. It depends how long I'm actually unemployed for. The thing is about getting jobs over here, they say you can't get in a job without experience, and the only way you can get experience is by having a job. So I thought I might go abroad and get some experience, then come back hand say, 'Look, I've got experience'. (*Tony, London*)

In 1984, the rate of unemployment among new graduates from the universities in electrical and electronic engineering ranged between 5 and 10 per cent — a rate unmatched by any other subject area (*Employment Gazette*, October 1986:432). Nonetheless, these two young men remained unemployed. Part of the reason for their continued unemployment was, undoubtedly, racial discrimination; however, the non-specialised nature of their degrees may also have contributed. Among the six graduates in this study was a young white man with a polytechnic degree in Physics. After spending 18 months qualified but unemployed, Ray went on a MSC-sponsored BTEC/HNC electronic engineering course for science graduates in order to obtain more specialised training. Interviewed within three months of completion of this course, Ray's expectations of finding employment were high:

> *Interviewer: What do you think your chances of finding a job are?* They are reasonably good, but if I don't find one in the next two or three months I will be a bit depressed, I think. The longer you go without a job, the less likely you are to get a job. . . Before, it was a general course [his degree] and there was nothing specific to aim for, but now I have a bit more specific training in electronics and there are jobs I can actually aim for. . . computers and their scientific application and control and monitoring, perhaps robotics and that kind of thing. . . the previous qualification was just an average mark and this time I went for a good mark to really have something to show. (*Ray, Sheffield*)

The remaining three graduates were women. At interviews, one of these women had found success in her chosen field, and was employed teaching and playing the cello. The other two, however, had yet to make use of their qualifications. Five years' study leading to a degree in dress designing failed to bring success to the following woman, who was now willing to try anything in order to get a job:

> Everywhere I went, of course, they wanted experience which is what they always do if you do designing. You can understand, nobody was willing to take me on and train me, I found it very hard once I had left college. . .I thought with these qualifications I can't be that bad. I studied hard for it and it didn't come. . .Well, I would put my hand to anything if I were asked to. I have gone for other jobs, like shop assistant; I've gone for cleaning jobs; I've done a bit of bar work, so really, I've done all sorts of things. . .since leaving college it's been 2 years unemployed, all but eight months when I was working in a machining factory doing machining. It wasn't my thing and I wasn't really competent at it so I ended up leaving there. . .I think in designing itself at the moment, I wouldn't have a lot of chance because I haven't had the experience. . .I think other jobs would probably come a bit easier, say less skillful jobs like cleaning or bar work, but the designing side, not at the moment. (*Sue, Manchester*)

It is possible that Sue will be able to salvage the five years' investment she had made in a career in design, as she has hopes of self-employment through the Enterprise Scheme if she can manage to save the necessary £1,000. But where Sue might yet succeed, lack of success in the science field had resulted in a change of career direction for the last young graduate to be discussed. Kathy was a young woman from Manchester who graduated at age 21 with a science degree and hoped for work as a lab technician:

> After school I went to the polytechnic and got a degree in science. I was 21. I came out and looked for a job, but I couldn't get one so I did a lot of voluntary work and I ended up a year later getting a job as a play-worker. It wasn't the sort of thing I was expecting to do when I left, but I was happy. I was looking for a job as a technician in a lab and I just couldn't find anything.

Working with children influenced Kathy's plans for her future, and in the week prior to the interviews she had just completed a post-graduate teacher training course. Thus, although still unemployed, she is now looking in new directions for work.

The problems facing the highly qualified in unemployment differ in some important respects from those confronting the poorly qualified or unqualified. On the one hand, one can say that higher level qualifications should provide clear advantages in the labour market, hence time spent in unemployment should tend to be of relatively short duration — unless, of course, one is discriminated against on the basis of colour. Therefore, most graduates can look forward to employment within a reasonable length of time. On the other hand, if unemployment occurs or continues into years rather than months, not only are the skills and knowledge acquired in university or college likely to be lost for good, but the social and personal costs of this loss are likely to be high indeed. After all, such young people have done what was expected of them: they have trained; they have acquired skills and knowledge; they have looked for work. What else should they do? And for some, when the search for work is unsuccessful, social ridicule or personal isolation is the reward which their qualifications bring:

> I think that sometimes when you're out with friends it can crop up in conversation. If they are chatting together, they'll say: 'Oh, Sue hasn't got a job'; or people will say: 'You went to college — what a waste of time, you haven't got a job now'. Sometimes you feel that — was it worth it? I say I hope it's not been a waste of time but hopefully eventually something will come out of it. (*Sue, Manchester*)

> I feel different in some ways because I have got a lot of friends around here who are employed, but I am supposed to be one of the bright ones

and I can't get a job, so I feel a bit isolated in that respect. (*Ray, Sheffield*)

The rewards from employment that further education can bring are greater than those available to the poorly qualified; however, the words of these two young people make it clear that failure in the labour market carries a special price for the highly qualified.

Direct questioning about social class and family origins did not form part of the present research. Nevertheless, it is clear from their interviews that the majority of the young, highly educated men and women discussed above are *educationally upwardly-mobile* from working-class homes. Whether they will also be occupationally upwardly-mobile remains to be seen. However, among the group of young unemployed studied were 5 young people who had been brought up in middle-class homes, enjoying very different advantages in comparison with the other young men and women of this study. These middle-class young men and women provide a contrast to the others in what they expect from work and in how they cope without work.

Middle-class kids
One of the clearest differences between workers at the top and bottom of the occupational hierarchy is the way in which occupational identity becomes part of the self-image of those at the top. Achievement in professional or higher-level white-collar occupations provides incumbents with the basis for self-esteem, personal pride and self-confidence, as well as offering considerable financial security. Moreover, employees in professional and higher-level occupations are often differentially protected from unemployment and thus experience both less frequent and shorter amounts of joblessness (Sinfield, 1981). However, when unemployment does strike those in the upper reaches of the occupational hierarchy, self-identity may well come under threat (Fineman, 1983); and although most of the middle-class men and women in this study are still too young to have fully established occupational identities, hints of threats to these potential identities may nonetheless be found in their interviews:

Interviewer: Did you ever worry about not having a job? No, not really. I did a bit, but I knew that I would get work in the end because I was determined to and unless you do absolutely nothing as a musician you are bound to. I don't know, perhaps we are not all optimists, but I always believed that I would get work because I knew that I could, and I knew that it was a question of time rather than — I didn't think it was lack of talent, it was lack of experience, the fact that I had to plug myself and get myself known to people. . . I am very lucky being a musician in that I have always had a certain discipline right from childhood because I had to practise a certain number of hours every day, so that I never have time, I just know what to do with my time . . . I have had a very structured type of upbringing, but I imagine that if you don't have that, it is very easy to — I mean, there must be a complete void. If I had my cello taken away I would find it very difficult to know what to do with my time, so I completely sympathise with people who haven't had a vocation. (*Sarah, London*)

Sarah was unemployed for two years following her music degree, but was engaged in a mixture of playing and teaching when interviewed. She was helped in her search for work by her professionally employed father, who placed advertisements for her at universities and other appropriate places during his work-related travels throughout the country. Sarah's identification with her music and with her music career, and her determination to succeed were clear throughout her interview. Her self-confidence doubtless stems from the fact that she had finally begun to experience some career success when interviewed. In contrast, the following young man had still to find success in his chosen field, the theatre, but like Sarah, saw little separation of self and work:

Interviewer: Do you think it's important for people to have jobs in order for them to feel worthwhile or useful? That's rather patronising. I suppose yes it is, yes. But then again, you can feel just as un-worthwhile if you're in a job that isn't right for you, if you see what I mean. . . [I'd like to be] Director of the National Theatre. Because you've got a load of theatres there and you can actually create. I mean, I don't believe in commercialism but, at the same time, it's a great opportunity. . . My work is my hobby as much as my work. . . Actually, I do see myself working by the time I'm 30, because I do expect some work to come in because I've just — I did a television programme — a series of yesterday. So I do expect something to happen. It may take a few months to get round to it. Next year I should think. It's going to be a kids' series. . . If I'm unemployed, it's going to get terribly difficult. *What do you think your chances are of finding a job?* I don't know. I really don't know. (*Paul, London*)

These two young people share similar social backgrounds and similar identification of self-worth with career success. Perhaps if Sarah had been interviewed before she began to achieve some success, the same slight doubt about the future expressed by Paul would have been found in her interview. The three other young people of middle-class origins had not yet chosen their ultimate careers: Jason, a young Black of West Indian origin, hoped to find work helping young offenders; Michael gave up a career in management in order to come to London; and Katje was temporarily out of the labour force caring for her young daughter. Jason and

Michael are discussed in detail in Chapter 5 and Katje in Chapter 4. Perhaps because these three had not yet adopted careers for themselves, they did not equate achievement at work with self-esteem in the same way as the two other middle-class young people. However, the ways in which all five coped with unemployment reveal their separateness from the majority of the young unemployed. In particular, these young people had more resources, personal and sometimes financial, to fall back upon — resources which are denied to the bulk of young people on the dole. Katje, whose husband was a student, described how she coped with unemployment, and her expectations for the future:

> Piano is one of the best ways to get rid of emotions. One feels a bit happier banging away on the piano. Drawing is very good. It's expression. You feel as though you're doing something. If I could I would like to do my own drawings and sell them. That's something in the future. You can always improve yourself with things like that. . . I hope that I'm accepted for this counselling job and that my husband gets a job, a career, and we move out into our own house. I want more in life. We're quite young now, so what we've got, we already see it as a start. When you are older you want to have more things. This is also because my own family in Belgium always built up their lives. They all have jobs and they're all improved. They can afford things. The older they get, the bigger houses they get and they change cars. I don't want to stay behind. (*Katje, Manchester*)

Katje's ways of coping with her joblessness were not very different from Sarah's — music and art. Sarah described how she spent her days before starting work:

> Well, I went to concerts quite a lot because the GLC ran something that if you turn up with an unemployment card, you can get tickets very cheaply, so I did that quite often. And I went to friends for meals, and I made a lot of things . . . I would go to Oxfam and a lot of jumble sales and buy of lot of things and make dresses. . . If I had someone who, as freelance musicians have to do, was working strange hours, I would go round and we would play music together or go off and see an exhibition. I did have quite a lot going on.

On the surface, the responses of these two young women to joblessness may not appear markedly different from any other unemployed young person with an interest in music. In fact, one or two others in the study spoke of their hopes for career success through forming bands. The difference lies not in an interest in music or, as in Sarah's case, the beginning of some success, but in the generally wider access to society and society's goods that these young middle-class men and women acquired with their upbringing. Katje, for example, speaks four languages and used to enjoy horse riding. Sarah used Oxfam while unemployed and the public library; with her father's encouragement she approached a well-known cellist and persuaded him to give her music lessons for reduced fees. Through their upbringings and their education, theirs is a wider world, as the words of Paul, the future theatre director, and Michael make clear:

> Typical day? I get up. I have a bath. Then I go out and get the papers and have a look in them, because we've got the Guardian, Time Out, Stage and that kind of thing. Then make phone calls. Then have lunch. And then in the afternoon, I would read. If I'm not working, then I've usually got some kind of project that I do without getting paid for — whatever it is. . .I am a member of CND and various other groups. I go to Greenham Common. I'm a member of the Labour Party. (*Paul, London*)

> We're all interested in politics to a certain extent. We like to read the newspapers and watch the news. We like to get the Guardian and read the whole lot. So do my friends downstairs, next door. Most of them are politically the same: central left. We talk about politics in a rational way. We wouldn't consider ourselves radical or extreme. . . I don't think I'm typical. Unemployment's really bad for people in the industrial heartland, the North, who have spent their whole lives working and suddenly been cut off. They're kind of useless now. . .It affects working-class people from poor backgrounds who can't find work — it's bad news . . .I've got a bit more self-confidence. I've got something in me to get stuff out of this situation — a bit of intelligence mainly. . . You have to emphasise that your character is suitable, because they [employers] automatically assume that if you haven't been working, there's something wrong with you. So you have to emphasise that side; emphasise that your life is filled up with pleasurable activities and you've been trying to find a job. Bad luck if you haven't got any interests and just like sitting in a pub. There's nothing wrong with that, but you're going to get a moral judgement. . . I'd advise them to keep in touch. It's no good saying to somebody who doesn't like current affairs to start reading newspapers, but they might start trying to understand things, by watching TV, watching the news. Getting involved that way. Self-respect. Utilise the welfare system — you don't have to live in a slum. (*Michael, London*)

In many respects, the boredom and worry of unemployment can be the same for young people regardless of social background or education. Nevertheless, it is possible to see through the words of these few men and women the advantages that may be conferred by a middle-class upbringing. These advantages can include educational resources which allow the young person access to a wide variety of activities and to explanations of their own unemployment; network resources which assist the search for work; and financial resources which ease the time spent in unemployment. For middle-class young men and women these advantages help make time spent without work less deadening, and more bearable.

Notes
1. It has often been suggested that one function of the educational system is to allocate people to different parts of the occupational structure. Grey *et al* (1983), for example, suggest educational certification as the process which links educational performance to the distribution of young people to specific occupational segments. See also, Banks, 1975; Ashton and Field, 1976; as well as the results of the 1984 survey in White and McRae, forthcoming.
2. One of the most influential studies on the link between educational qualifications and the employment of young people was undertaken by the Manpower Services Commission *Young People and Work*, 1977. See also Payne and Payne, 1985.
3. The advantage which qualifications provide for young people in avoiding long durations without work is demonstrated in the 1984 survey of the young unemployed.
4. The number of young people leaving school without qualifications has been gradually decreasing and by 1981-82 only 11 per cent of school-leavers in England were entirely without qualification, although the proportions were higher in Scotland and Wales.
5. Discussion of this trend is based upon unpublished work carried out by Michael White of the Policy Studies Institute, from whom details may be obtained.
6. See, among others, *15 to 18*, 1959; *Half our Future*, 1963; Banks, 1975.
7. European Economic Commission, *Chomage et Recherche d'un Emploi: attitudes et opinions des publics Européens*, Brussels, 1979.

4 LIVING ON THE DOLE

Introduction

For most unemployed young people living without a job means living on the dole[1]. This much they all share. However, previous research into the effects of unemployment has shown that responses to joblessness vary considerably; that there is, in fact, no universal Life on the Dole (Harrison, 1976; Madge, 1983). The aim of the present chapter is therefore to document the variety of responses of the young unemployed to living without work, through investigating their personal relationships. Few unemployed young people live in social isolation. Rather, like their counterparts in work, they have friends and families who share their lives, sometimes amicably, sometimes not. Moreover, the young unemployed share with all young people the task of getting on with life. Young people get older whether or not they have jobs. Sooner or later they think about leaving the family home, getting married, having children. And quite clearly, all personal relationships, whether as friend, child, partner or parent, may become more difficult for those without work. Such relationships rarely cease altogether, however, and exploring the difficulties brought to them by joblessless can reveal the many ways of living on the dole.

If it is true that there is no single way of living without work, it is also true that lack of money and boredom overshadow virtually all responses. The unemployed young man or woman who does not experience at least moments of boredom or does not wish for more money is rare indeed. Research has repeatedly shown that these two are the twin evils of unemployment for young people: too much time and not enough money to fill it (Roberts et al., 1984; Willis, 1984; Coffield et al., 1986). Boredom and lack of money may intertwine, moreover, to bring problems to personal relationships. It is difficult enough being bored when you are young and without money. But when you are young and watching friends with jobs doing the things you cannot do because of unemployment, being bored can add both pain and stress to friendships. Relationships with parents may also suffer strain. The young unemployed are usually unable to contribute more than nominally to their families financially. Prolonged unemployment can increase their financial dependence on their parents, while insufficient money may mean spending too much time at home and thus exacerbate feelings of boredom. Both of these may heighten conflict between parents and children. Furthermore, getting married and having children — both of which may ease the boredom of unemployment — may be prevented, or at least delayed, by lack of money. While if marriage, and in particular, children, do happen on the dole, the chances are high that the relief from boredom that they bring will be marred by the troubles which come from lack of money.

Living on the dole, then, means boredom and little money, and these two, singly or combined, may influence the personal relationships of the young unemployed. Documenting how they do so forms the remainder of this chapter, which begins with the young unemployed and their friends before turning to relations with parents, and ends with marriage plans and the already married. First, however, is money.

Money

Although discussions of money — or, more accurately, the lack of money — pervade all areas investigated in this chapter, its importance to the young unemployed warrants special consideration. When asked if money was generally difficult owing to unemployment, over three-quarters of both men and women in the study said that it was. Rather surprisingly, however, almost one in five said no, lack of money was not particularly troublesome, often because they had learned to manage what money they did have reasonably well. In addition to this direct questioning, money emerged spontaneously as an area of concern throughout discussions with interviewers in reference to job hunting, taking holidays, buying clothes, health problems, hobbies, socialising, plans for the future — in fact, in reference to virtually all topics pursued. However, despite the pervasiveness of money troubles among the respondents, few young people interviewed were living in conditions of absolute hardship. This was no doubt largely due to the fact that participants for the study were originally drawn from the lists of those in receipt of unemployment or supplementary benefits, and most of the young people continued to live or remain in touch with their parents. The study thus excludes unemployed young people living rough or in squats and those who have otherwise dropped out of sight of the various sources of support available to young people without work. Nevertheless, most of the young men and women had financial difficulties and for some of them, those difficulties were acute.

As might be expected, the young unemployed in the greatest financial difficulty are married and have children. This accords with other research findings (Berthoud, 1984; Daniel and Stilgoe, 1977; Smith, 1981), but as married young people living on the dole can be considered to constitute a special case of youth unemployment discussion of their circumstances is largely reserved until the end of the chapter. In addition, however, a few single young people in relatively more acute financial difficulty than most of the young unemployed of this study were interviewed. John, for example, lived on his own in Sheffield, having moved away from his parents more than ten years before. After working for one year as an apprentice welder, John had spent five years in the Navy. Since leaving the Navy in 1981, he had had two jobs lasting three months each. When interviewed, he had been unemployed for 13 months:

> Being on your own, you have to survive week by week. You see, one week you could be quite flush, because you get paid once a fortnight, and the next week — it's that week, that black week where you've run out, trying to get through . . . Well, as soon as I get me giro, a big chunk goes on fuel, especially in the winter. I'm on meters, you see, so I don't pay bills, and I've got to keep stocking me meters up all the time . . . and there's me shopping, that doesn't really cost too much — I never buy owt for meself now, clothes or owt — so, food, and I usually buy a couple of TV licence stamps. It all goes on this and that . . . I don't drink, so I don't go out to pubs and things like that, although I used to when I worked, when I was in the Navy . . . I just stay in bed until noon-ish if I can. It's more economical, because as soon as I get up it's really cold in here, I've got to put the fire on, although it's warm in bed . . . I cook one meal a day, towards evening . . . I'm only likely to go out to visit people or to places where you don't have to spend anything. I usually go out once a week. . I had a girlfriend a bit back and we've been together about three years, and in that three years, like, I've worked that six months, and it was just after I got made redundant from that job, like she went off with another guy. So the guy's, like, got a car, working, had a job for ages. I felt it was just because of that, really . . . It's the feeling of inadequacy and — it all comes down to money, really.

Winter obviously brought greater hardship to John than summer, and it is to be hoped that his finances improved with the weather. Nonetheless, living on his own on the dole meant a very restricted life: when he said that he usually went out once a week, he meant just that. The rest of his time was spent at home, often alone. John was fortunate in retaining good links with his parents, however, and although moving back home was not an option after ten years on his own, he spent each Sunday with his parents having his one big meal of the week.

John presents an example of the adverse financial implication and impact of long-term unemployment. Unemployed for all but six months of the previous five years, he had nothing to fall back on and was thus entirely dependent upon supplementary benefit. However, short-term unemployment also brings financial difficulties, as the following young woman explained:

Interviewer: How do you spend your £30 [benefit]? Well, £10 of that — £10.95 has to go on the rent — which I think is pretty disgusting because if you're on Social Security you can pay £3 a week rent, but because I'm on Unemployment Benefit — which is the same money — I have to pay ten pounds something a week. Plus I need to go to the dentist, but I can't afford to go yet because even though I'm on Unemployment Benefit I'm not on Supplementary Benefit so I have to pay for it and I can't — well, it's things like that that I can't afford out of my money. I mean, such things as going out — if you can't afford it that's just a bit of tough luck — you have to grin and bear it. But such as my dentist, and I wouldn't mind going to an optician and getting new glasses but again I can't afford it . . . I mean, when I did my wrist in it cost me £4 for bandages, I had to supply my own bandages; and then it cost me money for pain killers, you know, prescriptions — it's £2 a time now. And I think of my tax and my National Insurance I was paying — it was colossal on my wages. Yet now I'm unemployed I can't get anything. I mean I've got to wait 12 month — I've got to be out of work 12 month before I can see anything for all that National Insurance I pay out. I don't intend to be on the dole for 12 month. *(Kate, Sheffield)*

Kate had been out of work for only four months when interviewed, and her story well illustrates the money problems which can accompany the transition from work into joblessness. Young people in employment are frequently low paid; as a result, few young people entering unemployment even for short periods have savings to draw on when medical or other difficulties arise. Debts which were incurred while in employment present further problems when unemployed. Comments such as the following were not uncommon:

Well, when I was working I got a stereo on the H.P. I find it hard now, paying for it. *(Sue, Manchester)*

While I was in work, we had been thinking that it were a secure job, we took out a loan to get a car to get me backwards and forwards to work, and we're still paying for it, even though I'm unemployed. *(Vincent, Sheffield)*

Of course, making purchases on credit is often the only way people in unemployment have of buying goods they need, despite the extra cost resulting from having to pay credit interest. Several young people mentioned running a catalogue, while one young woman who had returned to work after several months of joblessness spoke of the pleasure of actually paying cash for clothes:

Interviewer: Does the money from your job make a difference to your life?
Yes, it does. I've bought clothes not on my H.P. — just gone out and bought clothes. It's nice to be able to go out with friends and shop with them — so it does make a lot of difference. *(Fiona, Manchester)*

Others are not quite as fortunate as this young woman:

I couldn't really buy nothing. If I did it had to be on H.P. or something — a couple of pounds a week. It got bad. *(Donald, Southampton)*

You have to restrict yourself to what's in catalogues so you can pay it off week by week. *(Nick, Sheffield)*

Even these few examples illustrate the financial difficulties young men and women experience when in unemployment: debts, catalogues, medical bills, heating expenses — all these take their toll when one is trying to exist on state benefits. However, it appears that there have been some unintended, and perhaps unexpected, financial consequences of living on the dole for some of these young men and women. Learning to live on a low income may not be an enjoyable lesson for anyone, and it may be especially hard if you are young and wanting to explore the pleasures of independence and consumer goods. Nevertheless, it is a lesson several young people of this study have learned:

I think [I'm] more easy to live with because I am now far more careful with money, having been at home and we didn't have money to throw around but we were never really without, as a family, as a child in a family. Whereas now I realise what hard work it can be to actually earn money, and in some ways that has made me far more independent. I have learnt how to eat cheaply and dress cheaply, how to live in quite different ways . . . I can understand what it is to be without. *(Sarah, London)*

I try to put some money aside each week for bills, say bus pass, have one or two nights out a week — couldn't afford much more than that, and if you were going out, you had to add up how much you were going to spend and have the exact money with you. Otherwise you'd overspend so easily. *(Charley, London)*

Actually, I'm really good with money. I am about the only person in the family that is — and I am really good with money. I won't spend if I haven't got it, and I'll watch what I have got — that's all there is to it. *(Kate, Sheffield)*

I used to spend it more freely. I didn't used to get all that much, but with being on my own, well, I used to spend it on records and clothes. So in one way, with me being redundant it helped me to find out what I can do, what I can't do. *(James, Sheffield)*

The stereotype of young people on the dole spending all their money in the first few days and suffering hardship until the arrival of their next cheque is often true, as the words of many young men and women in this and other studies attest. Nonetheless, it is also true that many unemployed young people do learn — however painfully — to cope within the financial contraints imposed upon them by their joblessness. In general, young men and women living at home cope best, as their parents assume responsibility for food, housing, heating and so on and ask only £10-15 for board. But even among those who have left the family home there are a few who cope with the little money they have, albeit with difficulty:

It's hard but you manage. You've got to really *(Mary, Southampton)*.

Lack of money, then, is a concern for the young unemployed — perhaps the principal concern of life on the dole. The best they can hope for is that they will be able to manage. Furthermore, lack of money cuts across the personal relationships of the young unemployed, sometimes with painful consequences. Keeping up with friends, for example, may be simply impossible.

Having friends

In the course of interviewing, participants were asked whether they had any particular friends they spent time with, what types of things they did together, and whether their friends were working or not. One aim of this area of questioning was to determine if social isolation was common among the young unemployed, and secondly, to discover what were the consequences for friendship of unemployment. Just over half of the women and just under half of the men referred to specific individuals as their friends, often referring to them by name. However, very nearly 40 per cent of the young men interviewed were able to refer only to a more or less anonymous *gang or group* as their friends. This gang or group consisted of other young men (and sometimes women) who they met at the pub, or in town, or at a centre of some sort. Usually this gang or group was seen only in one particular context or place, a friendship pattern not uncommon among working-class males (Allan, 1979). Often very little was known about the individual members of the group, such as whether or not they had jobs[2]. The vagueness in the way such friends were discussed suggests some degree of social isolation, but neither the existence nor the extent of such isolation is certain. When a young man says *oh, yeah — I've got loads of friends; down at the pub — you know*, it is not always clear if he is speaking from bravado, or if indeed he has lots of friends. The issue is sufficiently sensitive to forestall detailed probing by interviewers. For at least a few of these young men, however, the discussion of other topics in interviews revealed their loneliness and isolation.

Proportionally fewer women than men referred to a group or gang of friends seen in a single location or context only, with less than one in five women doing so. The same problems in interpreting these group friendships exist for women; and again, further discussions revealed some isolation among women as among men. Moreover, in addition to the men and women who referred only to groups, 10 men and 7 women were either unable to mention any friends at all, or stated plainly that they had no friends. The social isolation of these young men and women was clear:

Interviewer: Do you have any particular friends? No, not outside work, but I'm getting some friends in work . . . it's nice to meet people, yes. But no, I don't really have any friends outside work. *Interviewer: Did you not use to meet many people before? You know, when you were out of work?* Well, only down the Job Centre really and no, not apart from that really. There wasn't many people round here my sort of age group, really, that sort of thing, or they were at school or what have you. *(Ken, London)*

Interviewer: Do people come round here to see you? Yes, I've got a friend who comes round sometimes when she decides to come round. *Interviewer: Is she working?* I don't know if she is or not. But most of the time I'm on my own anyway. *(Mary, Southampton)*

No, not really. I think you could call my relations friends. I haven't really any friends at all. I meant to say relations really because to be honest with you, I haven't got a friend in the world and that is about it . . . I didn't go out; I mainly stayed in and tried to keep my mind active. I didn't see other people unless they came to the door. . . . I see a lot of my relatives on occasion. *(Steve, Southampton)*

It is relatively easy to feel the loneliness contained in these three responses. But the admission that one is lonely or without friends can be very painful, hence only a few respondents spoke so openly. However, other areas of questioning in the interviews allow the issue of isolation to be approached in a less direct manner. These young people were asked if there were days when they did not leave their homes and days when they did not see other people, and if so how often. Matching the responses to these questions revealed 13 young men and 13 young women who regularly passed their days alone in their own homes:

At the beginning of the week, yes, Mondays, Tuesdays, Wednesdays — I just used to watch all tele, you know — I used to become a tele-bug. I suppose it were just like the start of the week, and you get used to a routine. When you're unemployed you get into a routine of doing nothing and after a while I just got used to staying in the house in the day, and I did. *(Fiona, Manchester)*

Well I started getting up late. Round five o'clock. *Interviewer: What did you do until you got up?* Watched the television. *Interviewer: Before you got up?* Yeh. *What then?* Watched it until it finished. *Did you ever go out?* No. *Were there often days you didn't go out at all?* Yeh, you could say that. *(Richard, Manchester)*

I wake up and I get up and make a cup of coffee, and then I have a look if I have any washing to do or ironing and if I've got nowt to do of them I tidy up and then I sit down in the kitchen and watch telly. *Do you ever see any other people?* What do you mean 'other people'? *Well, friends or family?* I see me mum about twice a week . . . [I] don't go out Sundays, don't go out Mondays, don't go out Fridays — oh, yes I do, once a fortnight I meet my friend. I don't go out Sunday, I don't go out Monday, I don't go out Thursday . . . Unless I hang any washing out I might see some neighbours, that's it. *(Christine, Sheffield)*

Although equal numbers of young men and young women in this study reported that they regularly stayed in all day (and usually all evening as well) and rarely saw other people during these times (thus suggesting a certain degree of isolation), as a proportion of the whole relatively fewer men than women fall into this category. The men, in other words, were on average more likely than the women to spend their hours away from home and with other people. This accords with other research which suggests that unemployed young men have more active lives than unemployed young women, spending more time out of the house, more time with friends, and filling time more easily (Banks *et al.*, 1984:345). However, this difference between the young men hand women may be more apparent than real. As noted above, more men than women referred to a gang or group of friends, with women more likely to refer to specific individuals. Thus it may well be that many of these young men are only on the edge of having friendships — are looking on rather than joining in — and thus experience social isolation in a crowd rather than at home. It

71

is culturally more acceptable for young men to hang about the streets or in youth centres, but it does not follow from such activities that these young men have established social ties of friendship with their fellow lookers-on. The only difference between the men and women may be that the young women keep their loneliness at home.

Some number of these young unemployed, therefore, appear to be relatively isolated in their unemployment, despite the difficulties inherent in exploring this issue with respondents. But social isolation is not the only reason why young people in unemployment spend their days at home alone. Lack of money also keeps them at home, as does the employment of their friends:

> I try to avoid going out on the street because it costs money, you know what I mean? I find just stepping out of my house already costs me five pounds or something like that. So you spend less when you sit inside. *(Terry, London)*

> Well, at first, when I was first unemployed, I didn't do that much at all and I sometimes used to stay in bed until about one o'clock. But as time went on, I got so bored that I felt I've got to do something, so I started helping me mum, you know, around the house, decorating and that . . . I didn't see any of my own friends in the daytime because they were all working. *(Grace, Sheffield)*

For many young people, then, unemployment means more than not having the activities and income which work provides, it means staying at home.

A further area of interest was to discover if young unemployed men and women were segregated in any way from their counterparts in employment; whether, in other words, friendships of unemployed-only develop among young people. Other research has suggested that one way young people in unemployment have of coping with their joblessness is to restrict their social networks to other jobless youths and to create with them a common sense of identity (Banks *et al.*, 1984). In addition, it is reasonable to suppose that groups of unemployed-only friends would form, if only because young people without work have more time to spend together and understand best the constraints imposed upon activities by lack of money. In the event, it turned out that just over one in five men and women formed their friendships wholly or predominantly with other unemployed young people. Of the others, relatively more women than men reported that their friends were mainly in employment (approximately one-half versus one-third); while fewer women than men reported a mixture of both employed and unemployed friends (just over one-quarter versus 40 per cent). This difference between men and women probably results from the fact that many more women than men were in jobs when interviewed, thus giving them the opportunity to know more employed people. The friends of these young women may also share their relatively more succesful (than men) attempts to find employment.

Thus although friendships between unemployed-only do appear to form, it is the minority experience for both men and women. For the majority of these unemployed young people at least, contact with the world of employment through friends in jobs is maintained. The question which then arises is: does unemployment make any difference to the friendships of these young people? And the answer to this question takes us back, yet again, to money.

Money makes the difference

In attempting to identify the effects of unemployment on friendships, participants were asked the rather vague question: does unemployment make any difference between friends? If necessary, this question was followed with one which asked if the young person felt it was hard for someone who was not working to be friends with someone who was. In addition, participants were asked if they ever found that being short of money made it difficult to keep up with their friends. Often, however, this last question was unnecessary.

The responses to these questions suggest quite clearly that for many jobless young men and women unemployment does make a difference between friends, and, moreover, that women tend to feel the difference more sharply than men. Just over one-third of both men and women stated unequivocally that being out of work creates differences between friends. But where nearly 40 per cent of the men said that no effects on friendship resulted from their joblessness, a similar proportion of the women said that differences arose *sometimes* or between *some friends* but not others. The women were, in effect, more willing than the men to allow that differences between friends could result from unemployment, and only one in five women said there were no effects on friendship. However, whether man or woman, saying yes or no, money was the overwhelming explanation for differences between friends:

> Yes, it makes it harder. Because you get people who are working, they can afford to go out, but you can't, because you don't work. When you do go out, you can only stay out for so long, because you can't afford to buy so many drinks. So, of course, it does make a big difference. . . .
> Yes, it is hard, it's more difficult than normal, because they're all showing you what they've bought and that's depressing again. That's the only time, really, that I do get depressed — when someone's working, when they're showing me, 'Well, I've just bought this and I've

just bought that or I've just bought the other'. That's annoying, that. (*Adam, Manchester*)

Yes, you've got trouble when an unemployed person comes to a full-time employment person, then you've got a bit of trouble. You see these people splashing money out and what have you, and they think, 'Well, we could do with that' and what have you. Even if you know them well, you could probably say, 'Lend us a fiver' or summat. They turn around, 'No, we don't like you, you're unemployed, you're not worth knowing' and what have you. (*Rose, Sheffield*)

Yes, very much so. Yes, it's not like — when you were a kid, you didn't have any money, but nobody had money anyway, you could think of things to do without money. But when your friends are working, they've got money — you can't afford to do anything, you're stuck. (*Charley, London*)

Very hard. Well, close friends, no. But friends that you've met through friends, it's hard to, you know — oh, I can't explain it — you know, when they're going out and they expect you to be able to do everything that they can do. So when you say no, you can't, they don't understand. That makes it hard. (*Eileen, Manchester*)

The strength of feeling and the power of money to disrupt friendship are both clear in the words of the young people quoted above. It has been said that equality of status — and with that equality the ability to reciprocate like for like, favour for favour — are necessary components of friendship (Dixon, 1976). These young men and women illustrate the consequences of inequality.

However, even those who felt that unemployment did not make a difference between friends referred to money:

No, my friendships never changed. My friends are my friends. I mean, they never went against me or they never said because I'm not working, no — I mean, my friends helped me out when I was on the dole, moneywise, you know. They said to me, 'Don't worry about it, here's a fiver, give it back to me when you've got it' You know, if they knew they were going out to midnight, 'The boys are going out' they'd say 'Are you coming along?' I'd say, 'No, boys, I can't make it'. You know what I mean? My mate'd say, 'Here's a fiver, come on'. I mean, you know, that's what friends are. That's the kind of friends — that's what I mean — doesn't matter I was out of work — they helped me along. (*Baljit, Southampton*)

Well, I've not found that it does. Because although me friends have got jobs now, they have been unemployed before, so they know what it's like, so it really doesn't make an awful lot of difference . . . I seem to find that they have more money, they're earning a lot of money, but they always seem to be spending it more. So they're always owing it to various people. They always seem to be just as skint as I am. (*Jean, Sheffield*)

It doesn't make a difference as though they reject you, but it might bring you closer together as friends because I think they do take — not pity on you, but they do realise that you haven't got money to spend, and they ask you if you want a drink and buy you drinks, like, which makes you feel guilty inside because you know you can't afford to buy them one back. But once you, if you say 'No, I don't want one because I'll not be able to get you one back', they'll say 'That don't matter, it'll be all right'. So they're good . . . It's not the fact that you're in work or you're out of work that makes friends, it's the way you are. (*Martin, Sheffield*)

Not having enough money clearly pervades the relationships these un-employed young men and women have with their friends. As expected, lack of money disrupts and may even distort friendships. And even when friendship survives, and sometimes grows stronger, money remains an issue between friends. However, the work done by Coffield and his associates (1986) suggests that an important consequence of joblessness is that lack of money prevents unemployed young people from participating in the social world of people in employment. Nevertheless, as the words of the young people above demonstrate, this suggestion is not fully borne out in the present study. Certainly, the young unemployed curtail the amount of socialising they do as a result of having little money to spare. Nonetheless, many, perhaps most, continue to socialise and do so with their employed friends — often with the help of their employed friends. Willis (1979) reports that unemployed young people rarely abandon their normal leisure activities, choosing instead to *scale down* such pursuits. This, rather than non-participation in the social worlds of friends with jobs, is the common strategy of the unemployed young men and women studied here:

No [problem] because, like I say, I'd rather go out and have one good night a week than go out and scrimp and save every night of the week. (*Kate, Sheffield*)

Ah, too expensive in town. Just go to one of the local pubs. Not going out too far. I'd probably go out about seven o'clock, eight o'clock, by nine, eight, nine, we used to be skint. So now, we go out for about the last two or three hours. Might be about once a fortnight, something like that. (*Robert, Sheffield*)

In addition, several young men and women reported having girlfriends or boyfriends in employment. In these situations, the person in work often paid for nights out, thus facilitating the participation of the one without work in social activities. By whatever strategy, most of the young people in the present study retained some social life and links with young people in work. Money is certainly a problem in relations with friends, but it rarely puts an end to friendship.

There are factors other than money which result from joblessness and disrupt the friendships of the young unemployed. Earlier in this report mention was made of the pervasiveness of feelings of boredom among young people without work. In addition to feeling bored, however, a few young men and women considered themselves boring — and thus not much fun to be with:

> . . . there is a strain occasionally. I think, you know, that person's better off than yourself [that is, in a job] and they have more to talk about than you have. You know, when you've been unemployed a long time, your conversation gets a bit limited. (*Grace, Sheffield*)

> It seems that they have less interest in what I'm doing, but I'm supposed to show all the interest in what they are doing. I don't see a lot of people, so I feel I'm boring in conversation sometimes. I think back on what I've done and talk about that, but nothing concrete about what I've been doing over the last few months, because it's all the same. Days become the same, unless you break it up and do something. (*Katje, Manchester*)

And a few feared that friends in employment might feel that the young unemployed were getting something for nothing, while the friends had to work for their money:

> they think you're getting something really fantastic out of it and that can cause misunderstandings (*Brian, Sheffield*).

Other factors included differences in energy at the end of the day, with the young unemployed raring to go and the young worker exhausted; and differences in attitudes to work, with the young worker hating his/her job and the young unemployed wishing for a job. Sometimes, but only occasionally, these differences are profound enough to break the chain of friendship. When this happens, the young unemployed man or woman looks to others in the same predicament for their social life, or, too often, just stays at home. But, as noted above, this is the minority response. For the majority, friendship on the dole continues, despite lack of money and despite hardship.

Living at home

Unless tragedy intervenes, young children grow to become teenagers, and teenagers grow into adults. Normally, at some point during the transition from child to adult, young men and women get jobs and, sooner or later, leave their parents' homes. Is prolonged youth unemployment a tragedy, in the sense that it disrupts the normal, expected transition to adulthood through employment? Does prolonged youth unemployment disrupt, or even destroy, the relationships between parents and children? History tells us that the hardships which accompany adult unemployment are likely to reinforce existent family relationships: families who had good relations before the depression of the 1920s and 1930s became closer as a result of hardship; families with difficulties became more troubled (Jahoda *et al.*, 1933; Komarovsky, 1940). What, then, are the effects of youth unemployment?

Research carried out recently in South Wales among families experiencing long-term youth unemployment suggests that, like the families of the Great Depression, families in the 1980s are both brought closer and pulled apart by prolonged joblessness of children (Hutson and Jenkins, forthcoming). Unemployment is only one facet of the complex set of relationships called family life. As such, the general effect of unemployment is to exaggerate, not to create, patterns of interaction within families. The present study in many ways simply confirms this interpretation of the link between unemployment and family life. In addition, though, it provides an opportunity to look at the reasons behind conflict between parents and children when it exists, and to examine the plans the young unemployed have for leaving their parents' homes.

The majority of the young men and women of this study were unmarried when interviewed. Among the unmarried respondents, 47 men and 26 women continued to live with their families of origin; 11 men and 6 women lived on their own or with friends. As a percentage of all men and all women interviewed, the proportions of both sexes either living at home or on their own are identical; hence, in this study at least, the young women are as likely as the young men to stay with their families of origin or to set up on their own. Further, the majority of both men and women still at home lived in intact families, with only 3 men and 2 women in households without mothers, and 7 men and 2 women in households without fathers. An additional 2 men and 3 women lived with their mothers and step-fathers. All but 10 men and 8 women had at least one brother or sister also living in the family home. Thus, most of these young people had more than one potential source of support during their time in unemployment, although it is also true that the possibility of emotional support or comfort through the presence of other family members entails the possibility of conflict as well.

It is very clear from other research that unemployment runs in families (Taylor, 1983; White, 1983; Coffield *et al.*, 1986), and the families of the young men and women in this study are no exception: about three-quarters of both sexes reported that at least one other family member was also without work. In many instances the other family member in unemployment was the mother, but it was not always clear whether she was economically inactive by choice or through being unable to find a job. However, as one of our primary concerns here is the presence in the home of other family members during the day, this distinction assumes less importance. In addition, 9 men and 5 women had fathers in unemployment; 8 men and 3 women had jobless siblings; and in the homes of 5 men and 2 women, everyone in the household was without work. Other unemployment in the family can have several possible consequences for the young unemployed, not least being increased financial pressures upon these young men and women to find jobs. In addition, personal unemployment may reduce the ability of mothers or fathers to give emotional support or practical advice to their jobless sons and daughters (Taylor, 1983), while the presence in the home during the day of several unemployed children may heighten tension considerably. Conversely, personal unemployment can increase parental understanding of the problems facing their young sons and daughters and hence may lessen rather than increase inter-generational conflict. The following young woman from Manchester who lived alone with her unemployed father explained how this can happen:

> . . . he is so understanding. I think if I had somebody who was always going on about it — I know I haven't got a job and should be looking for one without anybody else sort of saying — keep drumming it into me that I should be looking for work . . . I think probably with me Dad, because I live with him, I think you get to know each other better, you know a lot more about each other, being so close, being with each other a lot. I think in that way, yes . . . a lot of me friends say, 'Oh, me Dad's moaning because I can't get a job', me Dad sympathises with me and I think he understands more. (*Sue, Manchester*)

Sue felt her father helped her to cope with joblessness, in large measure because of his own inability to find work. Moreover, well over half of the young unmarried men and women interviewed shared her feeling that parents could help them to endure the disappointments of unemployment and could actually make it easier to cope. Fewer than one in 5 young men said their parents did not make it easier to cope, and less than half of this number said their parents made it harder. Only 4 women felt their parents made it more difficult to be unemployed, by applying pressure of various sorts. For the majority, having parents helps:

Yeh, if I've got a problem like, if they weren't here and I couldn't work it out, I'd be stuck with it. They help me to work it out. (*Robert, Sheffield*)

Loads of times, I'd turn round and ask me mum, why am I out of a job, me mum would say there's loads more like you . . . [and] if you think that way, you get along a lot better. (*Rita, Manchester*)

Yeh, well, seeing as my mother's here to cook and keep the house in order and all that stuff, that's a lot of pressure off a person. If, say, you were unemployed and living on your own, you'd have to do all that yourself. That'd just either get monotonous or you just couldn't handle it. (*Terry, London*)

They just seemed to support me in an emotional way, you know. They were sort of understanding me when I got bored and fed up and that . . . It [unemployment] made me more close to them, yes, because it brought us more — we could talk more at the finish, so it sort of, if there's anything bothering us, we'll come out with it and say what's the matter. I don't think if I'd been working all the time, I don't think we'd have all got to know each other as well as we do. (*Grace, Sheffield*)

The variety of ways parents help their children to cope with joblessness is apparent from the quotations above; in addition, one very shy young woman explained how her mother assisted her by telephoning potential employers and by accompanying her to job interviews. And although the young men of this study were somewhat less likely than the young woman to talk about emotional support, and more often — like the young man above from London — referred to practical assistance, it was nonetheless clear that many unemployed young men need, and have, emotionally supportive parents.

The overwhelming majority of these young people in fact stated that they generally got on well with their parents, with only 5 reporting severe conflict. This does not mean, however, that conflict is absent. It should be remembered that for parents and children the years between childhood and adulthood are often highly contentious, whether or not unemployment is present. In an attempt to isolate the effects of joblessness on relations within the family, participants were asked if there was conflict specifically related to their unemployment. Just over half of both men and women reported some conflict over joblessness with their parents, with roughly equal numbers saying such conflict was frequent as opposed to occasional. Sometimes, open conflict was not the problem but rather just an atmosphere of tenseness:

Not all the time, but there were certain times I felt like that [underfoot] especially when me dad retired, because me mum had got us both in here all the time. She'd got used to have time to herself when I was at school and me dad was at work, she'd got all day to herself. I think it just got her down at times. I mean, we never argued or anything. It was just at times you could tell by the atmosphere. (*Grace, Sheffield*)

No one's working. *Interviewer: And was there any conflict between you, you and your mum or your dad?* No. He used to have — just muckin' about all day used to drive him round the bend. You know, stupid things, but never any arguments. (*Donald, Southampton*)

At other times, however, open conflict is the problem. This conflict frequently arises as a result of young people being in the home all day, getting *underfoot*:

Mother gets annoyed with me because I'm at home all the time and she gets bad-tempered, but when I go out to work, she doesn't get so bad-tempered with me. When I'm at home, I'm always in the wrong. If I do something, 'you've done it wrong, or you've done this, or you've done that'. If I have a record on, it's too loud or something. But if I'm at work and I come home and put a record on, they don't usually bother, they usually leave it, that's the end of it. But it's because I'm at home all the time, I get underfoot kind of thing. (*Adam, Manchester*)

Almost half the young men said that they often or sometimes felt in the way at home, and that it caused problems with their mothers in particular. Proportionally fewer women than men reported this same difficulty, in part because more young women than men helped their mothers with housework. But one young woman of Asian origin, living alone with her elderly mother, explained how even doing housework could fail to assuage the anger some parents feel towards their unemployed children:

No matter how much housework I do, to her it is nothing if I haven't got a job. I try to make her understand that I do try hard to get a job but I can't and it's not my fault. And I do try to behave at home, not to get under her feet . . . she would like me to get any kind of job, never mind secretarial or clerical or anything in a factory even. If I did have a job then I would be more respected than I am now. (*Fatima, Manchester*)

The stress which existed between mother and daughter because of Fatima's failure to find work was clear throughout the interview. The mother placed tremendous importance on her daughter becoming employed, despite the fact that the mother herself had never held a paid job. For others, though, it is the life-long employment of the parents, and the corresponding lack of understanding about the difficulties faced by young people in the 1980s, which is the root of conflict:

It's their attitude towards the working life — that they've always worked. You know, when they left school, they went straight into a job and they've worked all their lives, and they can't see how things have changed to now when there's no work whatever. So they — talking about me, whatever, 'You're an idle git, never had a job, so-and-so and so-and-so'. (*Daniel, Sheffield*)

I think they're beginning to understand more now, because it's been going on quite a bit and more and more people are getting un-employed. But I think at first, like me dad used to say to me brother, 'You don't try and get work' — it's probably because they've always had jobs themselves or been able to get it. But they don't appreciate how hard it is . . . they keep on this sort of stress — you get to a stage where you don't try as hard, and then they come in and say, 'You're not going to geddit by sittin' there'. (*Liz, Sheffield*)

Well, the family used to get at me about it every now and then. They just generally nag and say are you ever going to find a job and things like that. 'Are you every going to do anything, ever going to work again?' . . . I think they all said it from time to time. I think mainly my parents but I think my brother said about it as well because he was at school at the time and so I guess perhaps he didn't understand what it was like to be unemployed or what have you . . . I used to argue about it a little bit, you know, try and, you know, stand up for myself and say that it wasn't necessarily my fault and that, you know, people can't help being unemployed, you know, things like that. (*Ken, London*)

In Chapter 3 it was suggested that a lack of understanding sometimes exists between the generations in regard to the link between qualifica-tions and unemployment, with some parents failing to realise just how important qualifications have become. Here we see an extension of this misunderstanding between the generations, but now in terms of the diffi-culties facing young people seeking work in the 1980s. Where joblessness in a parent's generation was often, if not usually, the result of individual failure, joblessness in this generation often cannot be overcome by in-dividual effort. The failure of parents to understand this, as the words of the young people above clearly show, can result in considerable conflict between parent and child, and add stress to living on the dole.

However, although conflict as a result of joblessness certainly exists between parents and children, it is important not to overstate its extent. Almost half of both men and women in this study considered that rela-tions with their parents had not changed as a result of unemployment, and a minority felt that, if anything, they had all been brought closer. Moreover, conflict between parents and children can co-exist with feelings on the part of sons and daughters that their parents help them to cope with life without work. In addition, many sons and daughters recognise that they may well have become harder to get along with through being unemployed, suggesting that inter-familial aggravation does not always originate with parents:

> Obviously they [her parents] are concerned, so they ask and they're interested, but it's mainly me. I feel it's my attitude. When I was unemployed I was miserable and impatient, couldn't be bothered. When you're working, obviously you are doing things, things happen during the day and you come home and talk about it — you're happier. (*Sally, Manchester*)

> I think if I were at work, I'd get on with them a lot better because I dislike little things what each other do and gets on my nerves, don't like it . . . I'm restless, can't sit down for long and I'm jumping up and that all the time. (*Isobel, Sheffield*)

Unemployment is only one part — albeit a tremendously important part — of the relations between parents and children and conflict over joblessness is usually contained within reasonable limits. When trouble does arise, young people take refuge in their own rooms, go for walks, or just wait until the storm blows over. Family life goes on, in other words, even with prolonged joblessness. However, it should be noted that this discussion is concerned with young people who remained living with their parents. Obviously, if conflict was sufficiently severe between parents and children, young people would leave — or be told to leave — their parents' homes. Thus it is possible that there is an over-representation of unemployed young people with amicable relations with their parents among this group still living at home. The present study may underestimate the degree of familial conflict which results from long-term youth unemployment. However, it could also be argued that the high proportion of young people in this study remaining at home despite conflict over joblessness is an indication of the extent to which such conflict can be accommodated by families.

Leaving home

Young people very often remain children in the eyes of their parents until they leave the family home permanently, and may even remain so until they marry and produce grandchildren. Independence, in other words, comes to young people through breaking their residential, financial and pyschological ties with parents (Leonard, 1980). Prolonged unemployment of young people could be assumed *a priori* to disrupt, or at least delay, the attainment of independence. In order to test this assumption, participants were asked why they continued to live at home, if they wanted places of their own, and if they considered it necessary to live apart from their parents in order to be independent. Approximately half of both the men and the women still living with their parents reported that they would like to live on their own now, and a further 20 per cent that they would like to move *someday*. The reasons why the young men continued to live with their parents were almost equally divided between lacking sufficient money to set up on their own and enjoying the comforts provided by their parents. Financial reasons dominated the responses of the women, with several women mentioning the difficulties of acquiring adequate housing while unemployed. A small number of both sexes had at one time prior to the interviews lived on their own, returning to their parents' homes either because a relationship had failed or because they could not cope alone financially or emotionally.

Living at home can mean many things, however. Parents can continue to treat their unemployed sons and daughter as children, or can acknowledge their growing maturity even though they remain financially dependent as a result of unemployment. Less than one in five of the young men and women reported that their parents put any severe restrictions on their behaviour, and those restrictions which did exist generally concerned not playing music loudly and late at night, not staying out all night, and letting parents know where they were. Restrictions on behaviour were, in other words, the normal demands parents put on sons and daughters living at home. However, despite few restrictions, the majority of both men and women considered that unemployment does make independence more difficult. The young women living at home were almost unanimous in this: only 3 women felt that unemployment had no effect on independence, with 10 men sharing their views. Nonetheless, although unemployment was seen as making it harder to be independent, nearly half of both sexes felt that they did not necessarily have to leave their parents' homes in order to become independent:

No, not necessarily. That's just my personal view on it. I don't think so. I think being independent is being able to make up your own mind about things and that, but I think you can still live at home and be independent and do things for yourself. (*Ken, London*)

Some people might; it depends how restricted they are at home. If you're not restricted at home you can be independent without having to live outside . . . obviously money does give you opportunities, and being in a job gives you opportunity to get on [but] I don't know what you mean by independent because you can do all your own cooking and washing and be independent in that sense; it all depends if you're restricted or not and whether you can go out and if you are dominated.

It depends on what your circumstances are at home. (*Marcia, Southampton*)

I don't think it is necessary, I don't suppose it matters where you are as long as you're doing what you want to do. I would be financially more independent, yeah. If I'd been working constantly since I left school I would probably be living in my own place now. It's made it harder for me to move from home but I don't think it's stopped me from being independent. (*Patrick, Sheffield*)

No, I'm a lot more independent than quite a few of my friends who are living on their own. My mum's good and she does worry — she'd hate me to stop out all night without telling her, but as long as I tell her that 'Mum, I'm not coming in tonight', or 'Mum, I'm doing this, that or the other', then that's fine. I've got my life to lead. (*Kate, Sheffield*)

As the words of the young people above suggest, feeling independent while continuing to live at home largely rests upon the attitudes of parents, and of course, upon young people behaving responsibly. If parents are willing to allow their sons and daughters a reasonable amount of freedom, then unemployment and prolonged residence at home can be accompanied by growing independence. Good prior relationships with parents do not immediately disappear with unemployment, despite the feeling of most of the unemployed young people that joblessness makes everything, including independence, more difficult.

It is perhaps not too surprising that the majority of those living at home felt that they could be independent and still live with their parents. If they had felt otherwise, it is likely that they would at least have tried to live elsewhere. In fact, wanting independence and believing it cannot be attained while under the parental roof distinguished the views of the young unemployed living on their own from the views of the majority of young unemployed still living with their parents. Moreover, the few young men and women still living at home who believed it was impossible to gain independence while living with parents intended to move out as soon as possible. The views of these young men and women demonstrate clearly how important congenial relations with parents are for gaining a sense of autonomy while still dependent upon parents and how, in the absence of good relations, moving out can be the only alternative:

Yes, parents tend to be very restrictive. They tend to tie you down, they won't let you do what you want. You've got to be in at a certain time; they don't want you knocking about with certain people; they don't let you stand on your own two feet. (*Joan, Manchester*)

I don't think I'd fit in again. It'd be really hard. I just can't see me going back . . . We didn't really get on all that well, when I was living at home. I think we all make it difficult for each other. And moving away, it's like you look at a situation and you move away from it, you can see it better. It was like moving away from home — it helped me a lot, anyway. I don't know about me parents, I can't speak for them, but we do get on a lot better now. (*John, Sheffield*)

Interviewer: You've never considered moving back in with your family? No. That would be a disaster. Because I feel a lot more independent now. I can do what I want when I want now. (*Brian, Sheffield*)

Interviewer: When you were living at home did you have any conflict about not being at work and things? Yes, it's me dad — he used to have a moan about anything really. He's just a grumpy type. *Is that why you moved out?* Grumpy old sod — yes, it is . . . I'm better off out . . . Be in at twelve. Any later, the door was locked . . . I get on better with him now that I don't live there. *Did your parents understand how difficult it is to get work?* Oh, mum did — a bit. I don't thing our dad did. He's had a job all his life. He come out of one job — he come out of the docks and then went to another one straight away. (*Dianne, Southampton*)

Only 2 of the 17 young people living on their own were in jobs when they left their parents' homes. Living away from parents while unmarried and unemployed can entail considerable financial hardship. But for most of these particular young people, breaking away from conflict and gaining freedom to do what one wants when one wants, outweighed financial duress. This is not to suggest that all young people who suffer conflict with their parents automatically move away from home as a solution; nor that all young people who live away do so because of conflict at home. Rather, the intention here is to underline the interaction between young people gaining independence and the history of relationships which exist between young people and their parents. Where those relationships have been disturbed by conflict, independence is often, but not always, sought by breaking residential ties; where harmony exists, young people in un-employment can, with some difficulty perhaps, grow to adulthood without leaving the parental home. As Hutson and Jenkins (forthcoming) note, it is inadequate to suggest that youth unemployment causes family conflict; nor is it sufficient to suggest that unemployment prevents move-ment towards personal autonomy for all young people. Conflict, independence, and the experience of unemployment take place within embedded family relationships and care must be taken to understand the complexity of such relationships. Unemployment complicates, but exists within, a manifold of relationships between parents and children.

Getting married

Throughout this discussion of living on the dole, little reference has been made to differences between men and women for the simple reason that few such differences were identified in analyses of the relationships they had with friends or parents. This lack of differentiation between the sexes may be somewhat surprising, but most probably reflects the increased independence enjoyed by young women in the 1980s. However, in the final sections of this chapter — getting married and being married — marked differences between the young men and young women come to the fore. Getting married is an important part of growing up; and although marriage in the 1980s often occurs later than it did in previous decades, more than 90 per cent of men and women do marry eventually (Chester, 1985). Logically, prolonged unemployment could delay marriage significantly, as young people fail to acquire the money and goods necessary to establish a home. Unfortunately, there are no national statistics concerning marriage rates among the unemployed. However, the evidence from this study suggests that, for men at least, unemployment does delay marriage and in some cases may prevent it altogether. For women, the picture is less straightforward.

All unmarried men and women were asked if they ever thought about getting married; if they would do so while unemployed; if unemployment would affect their plans to have children; and if their partner's employment or unemployment would alter any of their plans. For the majority, the answers to these questions were hypothetical. Only two young men were engaged to be married and although their future wives were pregnant at the time the interviews were conducted, their marriages were being delayed until, in one instance, the young man acquired a job and, in the other, council housing was obtained. One young woman was permanently separated from her husband when interviewed, and was accordingly treated as single. The remaining young men and women had no definite plans for marriage, although they certainly had definite ideas on the subject.

There was very little difference between men and women in regard to thinking about getting married or seeing oneself as married sometime in the future: just over half of both men and women expected to marry eventually; about 30 per cent did not want to marry; and the rest were uncertain. Among the men and women who did not want to marry, a dislike of marriage in general prevailed:

I like me freedom too much. I get bored with fellas — like jobs. (*Ceri, Manchester*)

No. Why not? I know too many friends and friends' brothers and sisters who are now divorced and that's put me right off. I'd rather stay

Sheila Silver Library
Self Issue
Leeds Beckett University

**Customer name: Correia d'Alva, Ilsy .
(Miss)**

Title: Young and jobless : the social and
personal consequences of long-term youth
unemployment
ID: 7000455746
Due: 16/4/2015,23:59

Title: The psychological impact of
unemployment
ID: 1701565178
Due: 16/4/2015,23:59

Total items: 2
Total fines: £2.60
17/03/2015 17:27
Checked out: 14
Overdue: 0
Hold requests: 0
Ready for pickup: 0

Need help? Why not Chat with Us 24/7?
See the Contact Us page on the library website:
library.leedsbeckett.ac.uk

single. That doesn't mean I wouldn't live with someone, but I'd rather stay single. (*Adam, Manchester*)

I don't think there is any point in getting married. It is just a piece of paper — a licence to nag. Children? No, I would rather have these two [her dogs]. (*Janet, Sheffield*)

However, when it came to marriage without employment, the differences between men and women became clear. For the men, the picture was very straightforward: over 60 per cent said they would not marry if unemployed; only 10 per cent said their joblessness would not matter. The remainder cited certain qualifying conditions such as having adequate housing or savings. No men cited having a partner in work as allowing them to marry while unemployed:

Interviewer: Do you ever think about getting married? I used to, but not at the moment . . . It would be very difficult to start a marriage off on the sort of position I'm in at the moment . . . I don't think it would last . . . because it could come to money in the end. (*George, London*)

Yes, if I had something to offer a family, I would get married . . . but not for at least 10 years. *Interviewer: Would you get married if you didn't have a job?* No, definitely not, that would be impossible. Why? A lack of cash, sick of the sight of each other I suppose, it would get terrible. (*Charley, London*)

I wouldn't get married if I was on the dole again. I think that it would be a bit of a burden being on the dole, married. (*Steve, Southampton*)

The views of the men are quite clear in this regard, and although it is possible that they will be swayed by emotion and marry someday without having secured employment, from their present vantage point marriage on the dole was generally not wanted. In contrast, only 5 women out of 26 stated unequivocally that they would not marry without first being employed. The remainder either said they would marry, or attached some condition to marrying. For several women, having an employed partner was sufficient to overcome their hesitation. Men in employment are, of course, generally paid higher wages than women. An employed man would, therefore, probably be in a better position to support an unemployed woman than would be the case the other way round. From this perspective, the differing views of the men and women of this study make considerable sense. Men are not only expected to support their families, and hence should be employed; they also earn more money, and hence are usually able to support their families when employed. Moreover, underlying these differing views and expectations were the experiences of these young men and women as single people seeking the company of the opposite sex.

In the course of interviews, discussions concerning boyfriends and girlfriends arose in regard to money and socialising. Among the young people with such partners, little difference by sex surfaced. Equal numbers of men and women reported that whoever was in employment paid for evenings out, regardless of sex. Equal numbers reported that unemployment meant staying in. However, one theme in these discussions was brought up by the men only and this concerned the unattractiveness of unemployed young men to young single women. The first of the following accounts is perhaps the most graphic, but it is echoed by others in the study:

> I can't afford a full-time girlfriend. You just go out for a night and get one and that's it. Leave after night, just finish with her and that's it. But I never tell them that I'm unemployed. I just go out and have a good time and then tell'em that — see 'em again, and that's it. *Interviewer: Do you ever think — I'd like to see her again?* Yes, you do but you haven't got money so — because you can't afford to take her out for drinks and all that, 'cos birds nowadays — you really want a few quid to take'em out for a drink and all that lot. I just get one for a night and that's it — finish. (*Gerry, Sheffield*)

> But if you meet anybody new and they say, 'And what do you do?' — if you meet some girl and she says it, I always feel no one wants to know some boy who's unemployed. No future in sort of hanging around with him. It's probably not true, but you get that feeling. (*Billy, Southampton*)

> You do get a lot of young girls, if they find out a lad isn't working, they're not interested. They won't go out with somebody who's not working. (*Colin, Manchester*)

Thus, for some young unemployed men at least, reluctance to marry without employment is not only based upon a traditional view that men should be able to support their families, but is also grounded firmly in the reality of the reaction of some young women to male joblessness. Not all young women feel this way, of course, but such a reaction is nonetheless one strand of living on the dole, and one which can only contribute to a young man's hesitation concerning marriage.

Participants were also asked for their views about having children. Gender differences were again located between respondents, but this time, at least in part, in perhaps unexpected directions. More young men than women stated that they wanted children someday, with over 80 per cent of the men hoping to be fathers eventually in comparison with just over 60 per cent of the women wanting to be mothers. More women than men stated that they did not want children, with about equal proportions being undecided. When unemployment was introduced into the discussion, however, differences in the expected direction resulted, with twice as many men as women saying that their decision to have children would be affected by their own joblessness, and nearly half the women saying that it would be their partner's joblessless which affected this decision rather than their own. These responses again make considerable sense in light of the fact that women usually stay at home to care for dependent children. What is perhaps surprising is the small impact that the experience of unemployment was having on the views of these young people about the traditional division of childcare responsibilities:

Interviewer: Would being out of work make any difference to wanting to have children or not? Not really, as long as you could afford it with your husband's wages it would be all right, as long as you didn't have too many. *What if your husband was unemployed?* Oh no, I wouldn't have children then . . . I wouldn't marry him while he was out of work. (*Stephanie, London*)

The only time I would be prepared to have children is if I was financially well off and that I could give them everything. *Interviewer: Would you have a child if your husband was unemployed?* No. Well, it depends on the financial situation. *Would you consider working while he stayed at home to look after a child?* No. (*Joan, Manchester*)

No, I think you can get married if you're unemployed. But it's not fair on a child, to bring a child up on the breadline. You shouldn't have a child. It's only going to be a burden on the state. (*Michael, London*)

If I had no job, I wouldn't have any kids at all. Because I don't believe you should bring kids up unemployed because you haven't got the money to pay for anything. If they want something, you need money to pay for it. If you're unemployed you can't afford it, can you? (*Adam, Manchester*)

The views of many of these unemployed young men and women are, then, generally traditional: men work; women take care of children. Men's unemployment delays marriage and disrupts plans for children; women's unemployment is likely to occur anyway with the arrival of children and hence does not of itself disrupt such plans. However, in response to the hypothetical question: *if you were married and you had children, and your partner lost his/her job, would you go out to work and let your partner take care of the children,* the majority of both men and women were at least tentatively willing to undertake reversal of the conventional roles played by mothers and fathers. Thus it is just possible that convention is being eroded by unemployment, despite the little evidence gained from the views of the unmarried young unemployed in support of such a hypothesis. Far better than hypothetical answers to hypothetical questions, however, are the views and actions of the already married among the young unemployed. The chapter now turns to an analysis of marriage on the dole, where little evidence of change in convention is to be found.

Being married

Analysis of the effects of unemployment on the lives of married young men and women must take note of two important facts. First, men and women in our society generally assume different roles within family life, with men primarily responsible for providing the family income and women primarily responsible for the household and children. While there are dependent children in the home, married women's contributions to family income most often come from part-time, or intermittent full-time, employment. Secondly, the differing family roles assumed by most men and women are institutionalised in the state system of social security and unemployment benefits. Thus, after 12 months' unemployment an unemployed married man continues to receive supplementary benefit, but an unemployed married woman loses her right to such benefits although she may, if she chooses, continue to register as unemployed. One result of this is that married women become progressively less visible in registered unemployment at durations beyond one year. A second result is that while single unemployed people of both sexes are comparable in terms of their social circumstances, married unemployed people tend to be in different social circumstances, depending on their sex. Marriage on the dole, in other words, is characterised by marked gender differences among the young unemployed. The varying social circumstances of the young men and women in the present study who were married or living as married at interviews provided a striking illustration of these gender differences.

At the time of interview 18 men and 11 women were either married or living as married. Of the men, 3 were in employment and one was studying full-time, with the remainder in unemployment for durations which extended from two weeks to six years. The average duration of unemployment for the men was just over three years. Only 2 men had partners in employment when interviewed: one had only very recently established a home with his employed girlfriend in response to acquiring a house through his father's work connections, while the wife of the second had returned to paid employment one month prior to the interviews. The wives of the remaining 16 were not in employment when their husbands were interviewed and *had not been in employment for any significant length of time subsequent to marriage.* In complete contrast, only one woman had a non-working partner when interviewed and this husband was engaged in full-time study. Moreover, only 3 husbands had ever been unemployed while married: 2 for less than three months, and one for 12 months. In other words, virtually every unemployed married man in the study had had, throughout marriage, a non-working partner, while virtually every unemployed married woman had a working partner. To continue the picture of differing economic circumstances: no married men owned their own homes while 6 out of the 11 married women lived in owner-occupied accommodation. Finally: only 2 married women were seeking work when interviewed, 4 were already in employment, and 5 were economically inactive because of looking after their children. The contrasts in the personal circumstances of these men and women were thus clear and striking.

Not surprisingly, differing consequences flow from these differing circumstances. And even less surprising is the fact that the most important of these consequences concerns money. Because the circumstances of the men and women differ so sharply, each sex will be considered separately.

Married men

The financial hardships accompanying marriage on the dole become greater, first, the longer unemployment lasts and, second, when there are children. Almost half of the men (8) had been unemployed for the entire duration of their marriages, having married while unemployed and continuing without work through three, four, and even five years of marriage. A further 5 men, who had been married on average for about five years, had experienced unemployment for at least one-half of this time. The remaining men had generally been longer in work than out of work during their marriages. Thus, for the majority, unemployment had been an enduring fact of married life. All but two of these men were fathers. The two without children included the young man mentioned above who had just recently begun living with his employed girlfriend, and a young man of Asian origin who married only seven months prior to the interviews and who continued to live with his parents. Five men had 3 children, 6 had 2, and 5 had one child. Each of these three groups included one of the men who was back in employment when interviewed. For these men, then, it was not just a case of marriage on the dole, but of fatherhood as well. And the costs of having children dominated their discussions of the financial consequences of living without work:

> I don't think you can get any poorer than what we are now, really . . .
> food and that sort of thing. We have to spend quite a bit on Sammy as

well — clothes and that. Shoes are terrible, they grow out of them really fast. He's just worn one pair out . . . If I've got any money me first priority is to feed kids and wife. (*Fred, Sheffield*)

Just on bills, grocery and the kids. Us two really had nothing. I mean, we didn't spend nothing on ourselves. If we see something we used to say, 'Oh, maybe next time' — you know. When the sales come on, when the price comes down really low and that was the only time if you wanted something, you might be able to buy something. I mean, you know the prices of stuff these days? I mean the kids' shoes, we've just got the kids' shoes. I mean £9 for a little pair of kids' shoes for him. And they grow out of them so quickly. £9 for kids' shoes. It's wrong. (*Baljit, Southampton*)

When they're growing up, you've got to have new clothes, new shoes, and stuff like that. At present, with the money we're on now, we can only just afford stuff for them now, and as they get older, it'll be more expensive and it'll be harder. (*Martin, Sheffield*)

However, it is not just the financial cost of children which weighs these fathers down. Their inability to give children treats and holidays, or simply to allow them life on equal terms with their classmates, also causes distress:

It's important for me because I want to bring me family up properly and to give them things that they need and want, and the kids at school and things like that — they sometimes have to go and I know their clothes are a bit ragged and the others — and they get picked on, so I mean, through me not working they suffer for it as well. (*Andrew, Sheffield*)

Interviewer: Do you find it's depressing at times being out of work? Yes, sometimes. Especially when the kids go to school — the eldest girl — when her mates are talking — my daddy's doing this at work, my daddy's doing that — you know. (*Malcolm, London*)

However, although having children is costly both financially and emotionally when unemployed, considerable benefits also derive from their presence. One of the most important of these benefits appears to be relief from the boredom and tedium which unemployment brings:

Interviewer: Do you think it makes it [unemployment] easier — being married? Yes, it makes it a lot easier, yes. 'Cos with two children, I mean, there's always something going on. (*Archie, Southampton*)

Interviewer: What about before the baby arrived? We were bored to death. We used to think, we can hardly wait for him to come. Now we've got something to do. (*James, Sheffield*)

The only advice is . . . just keep yourself busy. Just take your mind off being unemployed. I think I'm all right, I'm lucky because I've got two children to occupy my time while I'm unemployed, so I'm lucky in that respect. (*Martin, Sheffield*)

Although there was little indication in the interviews of these unemployed men that they were undertaking a greater share of the household chores such as cooking or cleaning as a consequence of their unemployment, it was clear that having and caring for children took up much of their time without work. It has been suggested that young unemployed women look to motherhood as a way of establishing status and filling time[3], but from the present research it is possible to see how children can make unemployment more endurable for men as well as for women. Children take the mind off personal troubles, demand and receive attention, and provide a focus for the day. As such, and despite their cost, they provide a definite bonus for the young unemployed. Or, as one father suggested, they give a reason for looking to the future:

The obvious thing is looking forward to these two growing up, seeing these grow up, go to school. Apart from that, there's nothing, nothing really that I'm looking forward to. (*Martin, Sheffield*)

Children do not, of course, constitute the only financial burden of joblessness for unemployed married men. Money problems entered the discussions of these young men in many other ways, some of which have been noted earlier. Debts incurred while in work, for example, present serious difficulties for some of these young men, with mention being made of furniture and cars purchased in the expectation that current employment would continue, while, unfortunately, the only thing which did continue was demands for hire-purchase payment. Another young husband spoke of the nearly disastrous situation he and his wife got into with bills for electricity and gas. Now on meters for these essential services, he reported:

It's been hard, but we've gradually pulled ourselves up (*Frank, London*).

These young men and their families survive almost solely upon the benefits allowed them through the state system. None feel able to supplement their incomes through casual work, given the financial risks to their families should such illegal work be discovered. Parents help when and where they can, but they often have their own financial problems:

they can't really give any financial help because they need it for themselves. They can only lend me stuff because they know they're going to get it back (*Brian, Sheffield*).

Thus, for many — if not most — of these young men marriage on the dole brings genuine hardship. Clothes needed for themselves or their wives are not bought. Holidays are not taken. Social lives are curtailed or became non-existent. Moreover, as the time spent in unemployment changes from months into years and the young men get older, their chances of employment decrease while their financial needs increase. And for some of them, the time arrives when, given their decreasing attractiveness to employers, the only jobs on offer fail to pay wages high enough to allow them to come off the dole:

I was offered a job about three months ago, and the money was ridiculous. They wanted to pay me something like £90 a week and out of that had to be tax. We worked it out that by the time we'd paid our rent to run the house and everything else, we couldn't survive, because the social security are paying the rent and the money they give us, which is £59 a week, that's just for food, lighting, gas, so we can just cope. So if I had to pay me own rent, which is £40 odd, we'd be worse off . . . For me to take a job, I've got to get at least £170 a week, once it's taxed you take home something like £115, out of that we wouldn't have no luxuries after you've paid the rent, light and gas. *Interviewer: Wouldn't you be slightly better off?* No, it would be about the same, but I wouldn't have the feeling of having to sign on. (*Malcolm, London*)

In work when he married some eight years ago, Malcolm had spent the last two years without a job. Now aged 27 and the father of two, his chances of securing work paying enough to cover his needs have diminished with the passing months. Given the obvious financial hardships of marriage on the dole, the question which naturally arises is why do the wives of these men remain out of the labour force? Surely financial hardship could be eased through wives' employment?

It is clear from other studies that wives' unemployment tends to be associated with husbands' unemployment[4]. Often this is the case because, in the face of similar local labour market conditions, work is unavailable for either husband or wife. In addition, the maintenance of traditional familial roles is important for many husbands and wives, and wives' employment in circumstances of husbands' unemployment would radically alter, or at least threaten, these traditions. All but two wives of the men studied here were mothers. Moreover, all but one of them became mothers either before or virtually simultaneously with marriage. Their time since becoming mothers had been spent wholly outside the labour market, and little indication could be found from their husbands' interviews either that they were about to begin looking for employment or that their husbands wished them to do so. Stopping most of them from seeking work was discrimination — in a labour market which offers low wages for women, and in a benefit system which deducts pound for pound all extra money earned above £4 a week:

> *Interviewer: Is there any chance of your wife getting work?* No, she has looked for a couple of jobs. The money they want to pay a woman now, it wouldn't be worth her working. If she went to work, the dole would stop my money and we couldn't cope. (*Malcolm, London*)

Given this situation, it should not be surprising that the only wife in employment when her husband was interviewed was joining her husband in the labour force, not replacing him. For the rest, joblessness for husbands meant no jobs for wives[5].

Married women
When the men in this study were being selected and contacted for interviews no notice was taken of their marital status. However, prior knowledge about the tendency of married women to remain voluntarily out of paid employment after registering as unemployed upon leaving the labour market in order to have children meant that differential selection techniques were applied to married women. Specifically, those women from the 1984 survey who were married, had children, and said that they were not looking for work were excluded from interviews on the assumption that, although interesting from many perspectives, they would be less interesting from the perspective of the present research. This assumption was reinforced in the exploratory interviews conducted prior to beginning the main fieldwork. Married women with or without children in the 1984 survey who said that they were looking for work, whether or not they remained registered as unemployed, were included. In the event, these selection procedures yielded interviews with 11 women married or living as married.

It might be thought that the selection procedures utilised eliminated women from the study who were genuinely unemployed. However, it is more likely that women are lost from research on unemployment as a consequence of the present benefit system which renders married women ineligible for benefit beyond one year without work. If one is ineligible for benefit, there is little incentive to register as unemployed. Hence, many married women looking for work fail to be included among the registered unemployed. In fact, one of the first questions confronting researchers investigating the personal and social consequences of unemployment among women is definitional: which women are to count as unemployed? This question of definition is commonly thought not to apply to the study of unemployed men. A man without employment is, within certain age limits, generally considered to be an unemployed man. A woman without employment might well be a housewife, however, and thus not be unemployed. Or at least so it is often assumed. However, behind this assumption is a particular definition of unemployment which equates it with the absence of (male) lifelong, continuous employment, and which is reflected in official estimates of the unemployed. As Dex (1985) points out: what counts as unemployment underpins who is counted as unemployed. As a result, the official count of unemployment among married women greatly underestimates their number.

The situation is more complicated, however, than simply the non-registration (and hence non-counting) as unemployed of married women who want work. For in addition, such women often fail to define themselves as unemployed. This is so for a variety of reasons, as has been documented by Cragg and Dawson (1984) and Martin and Roberts (1984) among others. For example, women may be unwilling to label themselves as unemployed because unemployment means *having nothing to do*. Few women with responsibility for housework and children would accept this as an accurate portrayal of their lives. Further, the stigma of unemployment can be eased by calling oneself a housewife. Or women may consider their wish for paid work to be futile, given the present level of joblessness, and thus see little point in labelling themselves unemployed.

More fundamentally, as women internalise official government definitions of unemployment, being unemployed may be viewed as the prerogative of primary wage-earners (husbands) and single people, or of those who are actively involved in continuous job search. Simply wanting a job — should one be available — is often not seen as sufficient reason for calling oneself unemployed. And yet, this is the one definition which seems to capture the full spectrum of unemployment among women, as was noted by Cragg and Dawson; they suggest that unemployed women should include all 'women without paid employment, who were interested, to whatever degree, in obtaining it' (1984:16). Although such a definition would perhaps be difficult to incorporate into official estimations of unemployment among women, it has the advantage of avoiding the kind of problem associated with narrower definitions such as that suggested by Marshall in his otherwise useful and sympathetic analysis of the significance of women's unemployment. Marshall reserves the label *unemployed* for women whose 'involvement in paid employment in the formal economy has been involuntarily terminated' (1984:237). Following from this, he suggests the following, though largely unasked, question as fundamental to understanding the interrelationships between women's domestic work in the home and paid work in the labour force:

> ... which women, if any, 'retreat' into the home and take stereotypically female domestic roles when they are forced out of paid employment, in what ways, why, and with what personal and social consequences? (1984:251)

However, this question is in fact quite limited. For not only does it ignore women seeking work who left the labour force voluntarily, and those who have yet to find their first job, but it also obscures a fundamental fact of women's lives. The overwhelming majority of women pursue 'stereotypically female domestic roles' in the home whether they have paid employment or not. These roles may be the reason why some women do not label themselves as unemployed — that is, they have plenty to do — but it should be remembered that such roles accompany virtually all versions of women's labour force participation — whether unemployed, or employed full-time or part-time, voluntarily or for payment. The question posed by Marshall obscures this by assuming a masculine model of employment and unemployment. For while the majority of unemployed men may indeed be in this situation as a result of 'involuntary termination' of employment, many women find themselves in unemployment *as a result of taking up perhaps the most stereotypical female domestic role — motherhood.* Thus, unemployed women may or may not have left the labour force voluntarily; they may or may not be registered for benefit; they may or may not call themselves unemployed; they may or may not be actively seeking employment. In all cases, however, women who want jobs and who would take jobs if they were available are unemployed women, regardless of whether they also do the housework.

On this definition of unemployment among women, only 2 of the 11 married women in the present study were unemployed when interviewed. Both of them were registered as unemployed — one because she had only recently come out of paid work and hence was still entitled to benefit, despite having an employed husband, and the other because she had only been married for three months and thus had not yet lost her right to claim benefit. Although this second woman had been without work continuously since leaving school six years previously, she would cease to be counted as officially unemployed at the end of her first year of marriage. However, unless she also gave up her search for work, she would remain unemployed despite probable non-registration. Of the remaining 9 married women in the study, 4 were in work at interviews and 5 were not looking for work, and would not accept work if it were offered, as a result of childcare responsibilities. These 5 women were included in the study despite the differential selection noted above because of changes in their circumstances during the interval between the original 1984 survey and interviews for the present study in 1986. That is, they were registered unemployed in 1984 and seeking work at that time, but sometime during the following two years had a first or additional child and withdrew from seeking work. None now consider themselves unemployed; they are homemakers and mothers, and will remain so until their children are older. All but one of these women had employed husbands, while the husband of the fifth woman was engaged in full-time study. Although this last woman was not looking for work because she preferred to care for her child, the low pay available to her through paid work meant that her family was better off if she remained out of the labour force:

> If I got a job and had to report it, then all the things that we get free for my little girl, and the rent etc., it all gets very complicated. We worked it out, we'd be working for nothing, we'd be getting less than we get from social services . . . I'm better off now, when I was working, I was living in a bedsit. Now that we have a child and the house, they are paying. I'm better off personally in a way. I miss working, but financially, I'm definitely better off. (*Katje, Manchester*)

The parallel between Katje and the husband quoted earlier whose wife was not seeking work because he would lose benefits if she did work is obvious, and is intentionally drawn. The differences between the married men and women in the study are stark: the men are in considerably worse circumstances than the women. Moreover, few of the women remain *unemployed* in the same sense as this word is used to describe the men (although in the past, the majority of women have experienced spells of unemployment both when registered as such and when not). Nonetheless, similarities do exist. And it is with these similarities in mind that the woman above is quoted.

The clearest similarity between these men and women found in their feelings of boredom and restlessness during the hours without work, especially before they had children:

> I used to get up about 10 o'clock, and then I'd do a bit of housework, then have a walk or go into town and have a walk there, something like that. There was no reason to get up earlier . . . I don't think it was so much that I didn't have a job, it was the fact that I didn't have anybody to talk to from first thing in the morning until tea time [when her husband came home] . . . I get fed up at home and I get bad-tempered because I'm stuck in most of the time anyway. [In work] I'm a lot more cheerful, more chatty, and I feel more relaxed in myself. (*Teresa, Manchester*)

> I used to be very bored actually, because we lived in a flat the last time

I was unemployed. It got so bad I was eating all the time when I was so bored . . . I did all the housework and then literally read for the rest of the day, or just go out looking in shop windows or what not. I found when I was working, I looked after myself a lot better, you know. I put on some make-up at least, didn't I? Sort of like, done your hair up and things like that. I think it gives you a bit of self-confidence in yourself and you take notice of yourself. (*Ann, Southampton*)

There is very little to choose between the feelings of these married women and the views of the married men in this study. Unemployment is boring. However, an important difference between the sexes is that whereas the unemployed married men have wives as well as children at home to occupy their time, the married women generally have either no one or only children at home. In other words, for all but one of the women, most of their time out of the labour market has occurred while their husbands have been in work. This difference has mixed consequences. Staying at home all day alone (or with small children) can be both boring and lonely, as the words of the two young wives above testify. On the other hand, if a husband and wife are at home together all day and all night, day in and day out, the chances of conflict are high. Several men reported feeling in the way at home and mentioned arguments which resulted from their being underfoot during the day. For a very few, however, being at home together brought not conflict but a closer relationship with their partners. It has been noted that the husband of one of the married women was unemployed for one year during their marriage. The wife explained the consequences of their simultaneous unemployment:

I think we're a lot closer because him being a 12 hour day and me being a 12 hour day, we've been able to talk more and we've been able to do things together, like going shopping and that where I used to do the shopping before . . . It made me more bad-tempered when my husband was working and I wasn't. With me being at home all day, there wasn't all that much to talk about anyway. (*Teresa, Manchester*)

Now a mother of two, this young woman found her time out of the labour market easier to cope with. However, it was not just women who reported feeling closer to their husbands as a result of spending all day together. The following young man got to understand his wife considerably better during the two years he had spent without work during his three-year marriage:

I think if anything it's [unemployment] brought us closer together. I know people say that if you see your wife day in and day out that you get fed up, but I think it's brought me and my wife closer. We can discuss things more easily. Because before, when I used to be working,

99

she used to keep — say we got a letter from — she runs a club, like, so she got a letter from the club saying somebody weren't paying their payments correctly and it used to affect her, she used to get upset. I know she were upset but she just wouldn't talk about it. But now, if we get anything like that, we'll discuss it together. I think it's the point that she thinks I've got enough on me mind wi'working but now we can share it, because there's nothing other than being at home to occupy me mind. (*Martin, Sheffield*)

Personal experiences of unemployment can, therefore, be similar for young married men and women even when there are marked differences in economic circumstances. Nevertheless, the consequences of differing economic circumstances should not be underestimated. It is banal to say that marriage on the dole with neither partner in paid employment is very much more difficult than marriage on the dole with one partner in full-time work. But banal or not, it is true. Sandra, below, described how life without work could be easier when one's husband was in work:

I prefer working and I would rather work than be unemployed . . . Everyday was spent looking for work. I had my son to take with me. We would go down to the Job Centre two or three times a week and you could see the young people, I mean of my age, who were looking just as desperately for it. Like I said, I had a husband who could look after me, but they never had anyone. They were just the same age, though they never had children, and I felt sorry for them. They needed work more than I did. (*Sandra, Southampton*)

Sandra's views are important because she was the only married woman interviewed who reported experiencing considerable financial hardship during her spells of unemployment. Sandra's husband was very poorly paid, earning no more than he would get on social security benefits. They had two children. Now employed for two hours each day as a cleaner, her income allowed occasional family holidays and, more importantly to her, driving lessons which might someday help her to find better paid, full-time employment. Nonetheless, she was not looking for higher paid or full-time work at present; rather, she enjoyed her time at work for what it was and considered that her main responsibility lay with her children:

We shall be moving into a house, so we shall have bigger bills, rent, electricity and gas, and as the children get older they will get more expensive. If I could get a permanent job, then we would be able to buy, but at the moment, my husband's wages will never pay the mortgage and the money I get won't cover it. Once the children are off to school and then I might be able to go to work during the day. But it will have to be something that fits in with the children because I am not going to push them to one side for the sake of a job.

Furthermore, Sandra entered unemployment, giving up a relatively well-paid part-time job, in order to accommodate her husband's change to shift work. His job provided the primary income; thus when they were forced to choose which partner would become unemployed, her job was sacrificed:

> He was on 6am to 2pm or 7am to 4pm and he said it was either taking the shift work or leaving the factory altogether. So we had no choice other than taking the shift work or else he would have been unemployed. My money wouldn't have been enough to keep us and I had to forfeit my job, so that he could work . . . It was either him or me and my job was nowhere near the amount of money of his job . . . It was either my husband or myself. There was no other way we could work it out. . because he is the breadwinner and it is his money that pays our bills and if it wasn't for him, we'd all have to rely on social security.

Sandra has been presented in some detail because she illustrates a number of important points about married women in unemployment. First, her employment was 'voluntarily terminated', in the sense that she gave up her job rather than being dismissed or made redundant. And although she did not do so in order to have a child, she did do so for family reasons — in order to accommodate her husband's employment conditions. Her decision was based upon rational economic calculation but nonetheless meant giving up a job she had held for nearly seven years and one which gave her considerable satisfaction. Secondly, for nearly one year Sandra remained in unregistered unemployment because she did not realise that as a married woman she had the right to register, and as a result she failed to claim her full benefits. Thus, although she was looking for work throughout this year, she did not exist as part of the officially unemployed. Thirdly, despite financial hardship and the extremely low wages of her husband, Sandra maintained very traditional views about the extent to which mothers should participate in the labour force. Other married women in this study share her traditional views, but apart from the wife of the student, they do not share her financial difficulties. When the other married women spoke of money it was in regard to their unemployment delaying the purchase of a house or a car, not preventing it. As one woman, now back in work part-time, put it when asked if money was difficult when she was unemployed: *no, because my husband was working (Rosemary, Manchester).*

Sandra, however, illustrates the other side of unemployment among married women.

101

It is clear that this research does not cover the full spectrum of unemployment among married women. However, as a study of unemployment among young married women it is probably quite representative. In the 1984 survey of the young unemployed, almost three-quarters of the married women had been in unemployment for less than one year, with the majority of them likely to be registered for benefit following childbirth. More than 80 per cent of these women had partners in employment. In contrast, nearly 90 per cent of the married men in the survey had partners not in employment, and almost 80 per cent had been unemployed for more than one year. The social and personal circumstances of these married men and women will differ markedly, as this report has attempted to document. Marriage on the dole is, in other words, a different matter for different marriages.

Notes

1. Some of the young people studied were in receipt of unemployment benefits; others in receipt of supplementary benefits. Generally, however, they referred to their money either as dole money or benefit money without distinguishing which benefit. The world 'dole' is used here to refer to the money received from either state benefits and is chosen because of its usage by the young unemployed themselves.
2. It is possible that the lack of knowledge some respondents displayed about the occupations of their friends or associates represents a *defence mechanism* of the kind found by Coffield *et al.*, when young unemployed men and women refused to discuss unemployment because the subject was too painful (1986:79).
3. There was in fact one unmarried woman with a child in the present research. However, although she had been unemployed for two years prior to giving birth and continued to remain outside the labour force, it was not possible to decide from her interview if she chose pregnancy as an alternative to unemployment, or if pregnancy *just happened*. It is an elusive tissue to research.
4. See McKee and Bell, 1984; and Laite, forthcoming, who is analysing data from interviews in over 1,500 households.
5. This analysis excludes the young man who had only recently begun living with his employed girlfriend. During the interview with this man, he mentioned the fact that the DHSS did not yet know about his changed circumstances, hence the couple was in receipt of both her income and his benefits. He was aware that he would probably lose his benefits when the DHSS became aware of his living arrangements.

5 SPECIAL DISADVANTAGES

Introduction
Previous research has demonstrated unequivocally that unemployment is distributed unevenly among the young, with young people from working-class homes and those having only poor or no educational or vocational qualifications bearing the heaviest penalties. In addition, however, discrimination in the labour market cuts across both class and educational qualifications, and may cause some young people to bear a disproportionate share of unemployment for other reasons. Young people from ethnic minority groups are especially prone to differential selection into unemployment. Further, mental or physical ill-health reduces the chances of some young people obtaining or keeping employment. While for others, past histories which include stays in approved schools, borstal and, finally, prison, result in prolonged episodes of joblessness. Young men and women with these disadvantages are at risk of becoming part of the hardcore unemployed, and as such warrant special consideration within the study of youth unemployment.

Ethnic minorities and racial discrimination
In most of the preceding analyses, the 11 non-white young men and one non-white young woman in this study have not been distinguished from their white counterparts in unemployment[1]. This approach was adopted partly because of the small number of non-white participants, but also because attitudes towards the labour market, looking for work and Jobcentres, towards education and re-training, and experiences with friends and family while in unemployment often appeared to be very similar, despite differing skin-colours. In one very important respect, however, there are differences between these non-white and white young people. Unlike white young men and women who find themselves without jobs for a variety of reasons, many Black or Asian men and women are in unemployment largely because they are Black or Asian. Ethnic minorities experience rates of unemployment more than double those of their

white contemporaries, despite being generally as well or better qualified (*Employment Gazette*, January 1987). In the present study, this has been illustrated by the presence of 4 young men of ethnic minority origin among the 6 men with degrees or studying for degrees. For these young men, even being highly educated had failed to overcome the racial discrimination inherent in British society:

> *Interviewer: Do you think that any groups are more hard hit by unemployment than others?* No doubt. I would have to be either a complete automaton or brainwashed, to turn round and say there wasn't, because I consider myself to be a conscious black person and without any doubt it is the Asian community, the black community, or any community whose parents when first looked at cannot be deemed as white. That is basically the straightforward way of putting it. In other words, if you can't be looked at and be seen as white, then you're going to be disadvantaged in employment. It's as simple and easy as that. I've had experiences myself, at interviews and sometimes on the phone, applying for jobs, and I think my accent obviously tends to give you away before you even get as far as the interview room. And I know that for a fact, I mean people might say, well that's probably a coincidence, but it isn't. . . things like that have a very hard pyschological effect on a person. But you have to be very strong-minded to overcome these things. I think to be aware that these things are going to be facing you in future life; it helps you to cope a lot better with it than somebody who probably doesn't believe that racism exists or thinks, 'Well, it's not me, it's the rest of them', it's that kind of attitude, you know. (*Winston, London*)

Winston was born in Jamaica and educated in Britain. Although perhaps unusually articulate when stating his views, Winston was not alone in seeing discrimination as the root cause of his failure to find secure employment. He went on, however, to explain how his parents prepared him pyschologically for living in what he called a naturally racist society:

> . . . so at a fairly early age, I was aware of the obstacles that would be placed in front of me, and I suppose that enabled me in later life to come to terms with the things I was presented with and be able to get that determination to be able to overcome and succeed. . . The thing about it is, that for a black person trying to achieve and get anywhere in this society, racism is such a part of the way of life of people over here, they do not even accept it as being racism, because it's so natural to a lot of them. You see, the thing about it is, that they really do not understand what racism is, because they are so naturally racist, that they can't understand what racism is all about. . . . And the thing about it is,

that when you're growing up with a life like that, knowing that it doesn't matter where they work, how hard they work, how much you try to fit in, how much you try to adjust, how much you try to be accepted, basically, you never feel that you belong, irrelevant of where you are, where you go.

Perhaps as a result of Winston's clear understanding of what it means to be a Black in Britain, he expressed little anger about the several spells of unemployment he had endured. Another young man, also of West Indian origin, shared both Winston's understanding and his lack of anger:

Interviewer: Did your mother ever suggest it might be difficult to find a job? Oh yeah, she's always suggesting that now, because she always says like, 'Black, that's what it boils down to, you're black man, you're unemployed, that's going to be the first type of obstacle you'll come over, like'. Which is true in some respects, that is true. You've got to live with that now, you've got to get used to the country, because there's people out there now, with all the recent rioting and everything, they're going to tar all black young adults with the same image, like. All thieves and everything and all that. . . [but] I don't get that sort of closed-in feeling, that no one wants to know you just because you're black or whatever, no, I don't get that feeling at all. I know some people like ain't got a stronger defence like some people, but my defence, I used to go to interviews regular, and you can tell as soon as you've walked in that you ain't got a job or not and they've said this, that and the other, and you've said, 'all right then'. I don't feel that at all. I think it's just, like, self-respect really. Once you've got that, then you just think about everything and you'll be all right, really. (*Leroy, London*)

Leroy had been without work for three years when interviewed.

In their somewhat diverse ways, Leroy and Winston expressed a similar response to racial discrimination — to the denial of work because of discrimination. They maintained personal integrity and self-respect and managed to create lives for themselves without work, and without anger. However, not all young men in their circumstances are able to face life with such equanimity. The anger felt by the following young man, also of West Indian origin and unemployed at least six times since leaving school, dominated his interview:

Interviewer: Do you blame anyone for your unemployment? If I put blame, I'd put it on this country, man, because this country's not organised. To me, this country's for rich people, they don't care about the poor and all this, they don't want to help no one. They look after their own interests, because they've got the money and all this, they don't care about other people. If they was caring about other people, this country wouldn't be in such a state. . . *Interviewer: What did you think of the riots last year?* Glad. Yeah, I was glad. It showed them people right, that people round here, people weren't taking the piss, people that had nothing, all these people taking the piss out of them, they're saying, 'Look, it's your turn to hold purse out now'. But now this country, they don't want to know, fuck people and that . . . This country's finished. I think this country is finished now. That's what I think. This country's had it. They had a chance to build up this country, now they put it down to the dumps. I think one or two from one of the [political] parties might care about black people, but the rest — they don't care two shits about black people. They don't care. They're okay for themselves, innit? . . . I wish I wasn't born in this country, to tell you the truth. This country, it's got a bad name now, and it might even get worse. It's bad. It's out of order. Especially how they're treating all black people, trying to take the piss — liberties, liberties. (*Lloyd, London*)

Racial discrimination, both direct and indirect, is the single most important fact explaining disproportionately high Black unemployment (Brown, 1984). The anger Lloyd felt at his exclusion from society and from secure work demands little explanation in the light of such a fact. Perhaps what does need explaining is the equanimity achieved by Winston and Leroy.

The men of West Indian origin in this study were interviewed by a young woman of the same ethnic origin. Perhaps as a consequence, racial discrimination was discussed more openly and more forcefully by these young men than was the case among the respondents of Asian origin. Nevertheless, belief in discrimination as the primary cause of their unemployment surfaced among Asian respondents as well. The single woman of ethnic origin in the study will serve to illustrate this belief. Fatima was discussed in Chapter 2, where her attempts to acquire work through acquiring shorthand and audio-typing to complement her diploma in business studies were documented. Despite her qualifications, however, Fatima had failed entirely to find a job in the five years since she left school. When asked if she found looking for work depressing, Fatima replied:

It is, yes. Specially when I'm coloured, you know. It's just as hard finding a job when you're a coloured person anyways. It's just that I find it hard to accept that, you know, you have the qualifications that they need and after you've been interviewed, they just say they've got someone else. . . the future looks bleak at the moment, no job, no future. I don't think there'll be any change unless I get a job. . . *Interviewer: What do you see yourself doing when you're 30 [years old]?* I'd rather not think about it — it's sometimes easier not to. . . I would say my chances of getting a job are less than 50 per cent. Being unemployed for such a long time just makes it harder to get a job. . . It is very hard to cope. There's no best way about it.

A recent analysis of the effects of anti-discriminatory legislation 17 years after its implementation concluded that there are no systematic differences between the overall levels of discrimination faced by Asian and West Indian job applicants, and that white job applicants are over one-third more likely to receive positive responses from prospective employers than are non-whites (Brown and Gay, 1985:31). In other words, Blacks and Asians suffer equally from unequal treatment.

The aim of this section has been to look briefly at the perceptions unemployed young Blacks and Asians have of racial discrimination in the labour market. Not all of these respondents referred to racial discrimination in interviews, but most did. Few condemned all white people or all institutions, but most expressed clear concern about racially prejudiced employers. For these young people, being young and black means being young and jobless.

Ill-health

Unemployment and ill-health often go together. There is considerable evidence that unemployed people tend to be less healthy than people in work. The causal link between ill-health and unemployment is uncertain, however, with some arguing that the former is a direct result of the latter, and others arguing the reverse (Brenner 1979; Gravelle *et al.*, 1981; Hakim. 1982; Miles, 1983). But whatever the statistical arguments, in a labour market characterised by high and persistent rates of youth unemployment, young people suffering illness or disability will be at a marked disadvantage in comparison with other young people. For some of these young people, ill-health will prevent or delay entry into jobs; for others, it will put jobs at risk. And although direct questioning about health problems did not form part of the interviews, instances of illness and disability were nonetheless found among the young people of this study.

Health problems can be either physical or psychological; among the young people of this study reference was made to a wide range of problems including ulcers, asthma, agoraphobia, dyslexia, allergies, depression and severe mental distress. Moreover, the consequences of these health problems are almost as varied as the problems themselves. In the cases two young men, health problems and vulnerability to redundancy had combined to create almost classical examples of sub-employ-

107

ment among young people, differing only through the presence of ill-health. For a third young man, ill-health and disability had combined to prevent employment altogether. A fourth was at risk of losing his job through back problems; a fifth, now in his sixth year without work, suffered from ulcers; while a sixth suffered more health problems in work than out of work. It is not readily apparent why physical health problems were referred to predominantly by men. Psychological problems, referred to by women as well as men, are discussed later in the chapter.

Work histories which comprise a series of short-term, dead-end jobs and spells of unemployment are common among young workers and examples of this pattern of employment have been cited elsewhere in this study. For the following two young men, however, health problems had contributed significantly to their fragmented labour market experiences. Colin left school on a Friday in 1980 and began his first job on the following Monday. He outlined what followed next:

> I just took that job because it was offered. It lasted two months. I left because I had a dust allergy. I didn't know at the time, but I had to leave for health reasons. Then I was on the dole for about three months. Then I got a job as a carpet-fitter and stayed working there for seven months until the firm went into liquidation and I was made redundant. So I was on the dole again for eight months. Then I got a job as an apprentice butcher. That lasted for three months. I left there because I didn't like the environment I was working in or the people. Then I was unemployed again for nearly a year. The last job I had was landscape gardening. I left that also, of my own accord, after a few months. It wasn't that I didn't like it, I enjoyed the job. It was health reasons. (*Colin, Manchester*)

In his current spell of unemployment for fourteen months when interviewed, Colin's work history reveals the cumulative effect sub-employment can have, with each spell of joblessness lasting longer than the previous one. In Colin's case, poor health compounded, but clearly did not cause, a precarious attachment to the labour force.

On the surface, Billy's working history also presents a classic example of sub-employment among young people. He had held a series of poorly-paid, unskilled jobs in warehouses, pizza restaurants and food-stores interspersed with spells of joblessness. However, Billy differed from other young people in the labour market in that he suffered from dyslexia and attended a special school because of his reading problems. Billy was once again in unemployment when interviewed; and in his interview, he mentioned past jobs held and then lost as a result of his getting confused at work:

> . . . I had a lot of trouble with the till — it was all computerised num-

bers and I got made redund- I got sacked from there. . . Then I was employed in a warehouse job. I thought, 'Here we go, the ideal job' but then that turned out to be clerical and I had to do a lot of writing and I wasn't very good at remembering these six figure numbers . . . [another] job I stayed in for about three months, I think, and — I don't know, the boss there was very panicky — it was confusing, he would say, 'Lock all the cars up', and you'd lock all the cars up and then he would say, 'This one and not this one'. (*Billy, Southampton*).

A work accident in which Billy cracked his pelvis put an end to yet another job.

Despite the difficulty Billy had in keeping the jobs he found, he had at least been fortunate enough to find some work. He described the problems dyslexia caused him in his search for secure employment:

. . . most people don't know what it means! And some people don't believe it's — it's just a made up thing so you have an excuse. I couldn't tell the time for a long time. Couldn't spell my name for a long time . . .and when I've had these bums jobs, I were really quite depressed because you find, like with my HGV, some days I could do it and some days I couldn't do it and I really got frustrated with that because I thought this would be easy, but it's a lot harder than anybody thinks.

For both Colin and Billy, it is clear that unemployment did not cause their health problems. In Colin's case, spells of unemployment might even have eased his allergy as he was no longer required to spend several hours a day in dusty environments. However, for both these young men, and for Billy in particular, health problems certainly caused unemployment.

Like Billy, a third young man also experienced unemployment as a result of health problems and disability. For the first six years of his education, Alan attended a special school, living away from his parents. It was plain from Alan's interview that he was quite slow in his thinking and that his happiest hours were spent with his many and varied pets. In addition, Alan suffered from asthma and it was this which caused him the most aggravation in looking for work:

Interviewer: What is it you dislike about looking for work? It's only medical forms or owt like that, they ask you whether you had any diseases or owt like that, and you tell them about asthma, they think, like it's real serious. But it's not that serious, cause usually — I don't hardly get it a lot now. . . You still have to put it down through doctors or owt like that. I can do all sorts of work. It's just like if it's real summer and I get, like, hay fever, plus if I get a cold on it, I'm bad then. But otherwise, I've got these [ventilator] — sometimes I take that, if it's real bad, but usually I just carry on. (*Alan, Sheffield*)

109

In a labour market less marked by high rates of youth unemployment, Alan might have been able to find work which suited both his abilities and his interests. In the present labour market, however, he had had no success at all.

With these three young men, it is possible to see the ways in which disability or ill-health which pre-dates entry into the labour market can seriously affect a young person's job chances, even to the extent of preventing employment altogether. The following young man, however, was in work when interviewed. Of Asian origin, he had managed to over-come the kind of discrimination discussed above and find employment, only to develop back trouble of sufficient severity to require hospital treatment. And now his job was under threat:

> I've got this job now, but I'm on sick note at the moment because of my back. But I'm scared if I lose this job, what will I do next? But at the same time, my back comes first. I've been off for what, three months now, because of my back. . . Well, it's been going on now for what, two years now, my back trouble. But it went away and it keeps coming back. But then one day I was at work lifting and it was all right. Got home, woke up the next morning and a shock went right down my leg. The disc had gone. . .I am worried now because of my job, but then the doctor said, 'Well, you can't do nothing about it'. He said, 'If you go back to work and you lift a barrel or lift anything, your back's just going to go like that. And you're going to start off from where you were in the first place. That means if you go back', he goes on. 'Well, I won't sign you back on to work'. . .I'm worried about my job. . . I'm not 22 now, 26 now and I've got three kids. It's going to be harder for me now, you know what I mean. You know, he [his employer] said to me, 'Come and see me when your back's better', but that doesn't mean, you know, that means, might take you back on or no I'm afraid I can't. If he said to me, 'I'll keep it for you, Baljit, don't worry about it, get your back better', then that's a different matter. I wouldn't worry about it. But he can't say that because he's got to get the work done. I see his point of view as well as mine. He has got a business to run.
> (*Baljit, Southampton*)

The difficulties Baljit was experiencing and the unemployment he was facing are symptomatic of the conditions of work available to unqualified young men employed in the lower half of the labour market. Baljit was employed as a bartender, having experienced gradual downward mobility in occupations since losing his first job as a skilled woodworker; as such, his job involved moving heavy barrels and tables. If Baljit had been in non-manual work, his back would have been subject to much less risk of injury. If he had been in manual work, but protected by union membership, his job would probably have been less at risk. But Baljit had neither non-manual work nor union protection; hence, the back trouble which work exacerbated was likely to be the health trouble which cost him his job.

Baljit was not the only young man in this research to have experienced downward mobility in occupations, taking whatever work was available in order to avoid unemployment. Nor was he the only young man to end up in work which placed his health at risk as a result. Michael was a young man from middle-class family origins, but nonetheless had only poor educational qualifications. Michael's first job as a management trainee in a large retail chain store could have given him occupational security and a career. But after six years with this company, Michael quit his job, left his childhood home, and came to London:

> *Interviewer: What were your reasons for leaving the job?* That was about four years ago. I left to move to London. When I left work, I left my home, parents, social life, friends — apart from the one friend I had here. I made a complete break. I was bored. It was cosy, safe. I had lots of friends, lots of social activities, a regular job. I lived at home, so that could account for everything. . . I left not to stop work but to change my whole life. I hoped to find some sort of work [but] I found it more difficult than I ever imagined.

In fact, all Michael was able to find in London were temporary unskilled jobs such as messenger, kitchen porter, delivery worker and the like. These jobs aggravated his already precarious health:

> I think my health was worse when I was working. I used to get a lot of dirt into my hands and it would bring up an eczema thing. I had to put cream on. Probably because I was trying to do too much. I had a lot of illnesses, like bad skin, asthma, headaches, upset stomach, and general ill-health. I had about three bouts of 'flu in nine months. . . If I don't look after myself, I get all sorts of things. These are things which I haven't suffered half as much since I left work. . . I can't say I'm healthy because I still suffer from the eczema. . .Yes, it was dirty places. Really grubby. If I get anything on my skin I can't use soap. So you have to suffer the consequences if you clean the dirt off. The dirt got in my lungs.

Michael and Baljit suffered working conditions common to a great many young people in the labour market; some young people in the present study spoke of conditions that were far inferior. However, for these two young men, poor health was made worse by poor working conditions and although prolonged unemployment will doubtlessly harm them in other ways, it may also lead to improved health.

With the exception of Michael, the young men discussed so far have experienced, or are at risk of, unemployment as a result of physical ill-health or disability. Only one young man spoke of physical health problems which could be attributed to unemployment rather than the reverse. Married with one child, Tom had been out of work for six consecutive years when interviewed. He spoke about his problems:

[I feel] rotten at times. Feel like jumping in the nearest river or something. Also it affects you in all ways, I suppose. I have ulcers. That's just started about past three, four year ago. *Interviewer: You put that down to worry, do you?* I put that down to the worry, yes. The wife always keeps saying I've got bad-tempered and things like that, which I suppose has changed from when I was working . . . I never got bored with it, with working, but on the last job I was depressed with the job, but like I said, I stuck it out because it were a job until I actually finished. (*Tom, Manchester*)

It is possible that other young men and women in this study have anxiety-related physical problems as a result of their prolonged joblessness. However, none mentioned such difficulties. Depression as a consequence of unemployment was, however, discussed with all participants. Joblessness entails deprivation of social contacts and involvement as well as loss of the status and self-esteem associated with employment. These factors provide good reason for expecting psychological distress to accompany joblessness. The majority of both men and women in the present study (over 60 per cent of the men and almost 80 per cent of the women) reported feeling depressed about their lack of work. In part, depression results from boredom — from simply not having anything to do. But in addition, depression can stem from other people's views of the young person's joblessness, with comments and criticisms coming from outsiders and family members as well. Over one-third of the men and almost half of the women reported instances of other people making them feel useless or of no worth because they did not have jobs. And feeling useless and feeling depressed both make unemployment harder to bear:

You find when you are out of work, you get into yourself and tend not to speak to people when you meet them . . . probably because you're not mixing. You feel down because you don't have a job. You also get a lot of aggravation from your parents — I was told I was lazy. I didn't look for jobs. It was terrible. (*Joan, Manchester*)

Interviewer: Did you worry about not having a job? Yes. I wondered how it was all going to end. I had a job that lasted for four months when I was 20 years old and then nothing at all. *Interviewer: What did you do when you felt worried?* Just lived in a little dream world most of the time. (*Charley, London*)

It worries me to think I'm never going to get a job. Because I don't want to be unemployed for the rest of my life. *Interviewer: So what do you do when you start to worry?* Get depressed. *And then what do you do when you get depressed?* Get more depressed. (*Brian, Sheffield*)

I think you don't have anything to occupy your mind, you just gradually get depressed and you have nothing to look forward to or anything like that . . . I'd wake up and there'd be nothing specific that I'd have to do during the day or anything like that, and it would get me down after a while, yes. (*Ken, London*)

Feelings of depression were common among these young unemployed, then, with the young men almost as willing as the young women to discuss their depression. But in addition to this more or less generalised sense of *ennui* among the respondents, instances of severe depression and psychiatric problems were discovered. In none of these cases, however, can it be said that unemployment had *caused* the mental ill-health; rather, for most of them, psychological distress had been *exacerbated* by unemployment. One such young man, Pete, who considered himself a virtual recluse and who had sought solace for his problems in studying for a degree, was discussed in Chapter 3. As noted there, Pete realised that unemployment had quite probably made it much more difficult for him to overcome his mental problems. In addition to Pete, four women referred to psychological ill-health; only one of them was in work when interviewed.

Grace first began suffering from agoraphobia at the age of 14. She withdrew from public education, and was tutored at home until aged 16. From age 16 onwards, her illness began to improve:

It was sort of up and down. I seemed to get over it, you know, when I first started work at (firm) and then I had a relapse and it seemed to be up and down until I got to be about 19; then when I got to 20, that was when I finally got over it. *Interviewer: Do you think that that had an effect on your job opportunities?* Yes, because I think with lack of qualifications, I mean, it's not that I wasn't capable but you weren't allowed to take exams at home. You got to be in a classroom and I think that put a lot of people off. (*Grace, Sheffield*)

Grace suggested that her illness might have disappeared more quickly if she had been able to find work at the age of 16, for then she would have got used to going out rather than staying in. However, after about three years unemployment, Grace found part-time work in a department store and had been in this job just over six months when interviewed. Grace's illness and subsequent withdrawal from school clearly delayed her entry into work as well as rendering her unable to compete for the types of jobs her two university-educated sisters had obtained. Nevertheless, she was now well and enjoying her part-time employment. Sadly, the same cannot be said for the three other women in this research who suffered from psychological problems. None of them were in work when interviewed. Moreover, each had been out of work for more than four years and one for more than five years. It should be re-iterated that it was clear in interviews that these women suffered from long-standing psychological problems, which were not brought on by failure to find employment. Nevertheless, it was also clear that, in each case, the illness was made much worse by the isolation, boredom and idleness that accompanies joblessness. One of these women, Mary, talked about her life and her future:

> My future? Terrible at the moment . . . I don't know. I might be dead in a couple of years, put it that way. I don't know why, because I feel that way. I always have done. Because of everything, really, because when I was born I regretted it. As soon as I was born I regretted ever being born. I wish me mum had pushed me back up again. Because I didn't want to be born. And I still don't now . . . I've always felt that, you know, because, I don't know, my life's one big nightmare. It's not even going away at the moment . . . Well, it's like a horror film but it's not. You see, with a horror film, the nightmare goes, but with my nightmare, it doesn't — it just lingers on and on . . . At the moment I am fed up with life anyway. I'm just going down and down and down.

Mary, who lived in Southampton, suggested that her problems stemmed from certain childhood occurrences, and she informed the interviewer that she was in contact with a doctor, although not receiving psychiatric treatment. Mary had not worked for more than four years, giving up the few jobs she did find following school because of intolerable working conditions. Her pyschological problems were compounded by asthma, thus limiting the type of work she was able to undertake.

The two other women discussed here referred, like Mary, to the possibility of suicide. Rose, out of work for virtually all of the six years that had passed since she left school, did so obliquely:

> No, I never make plans; I just take each day as they come. *Interviewer: What do you see yourself doing when you're about 30?* I don't know. I might not be here. Well, if it carries on, there'll be a lot that'll commit suicide to try to get out of it. They've got no money, no life. (*Rose, Sheffield*)

When pressed, Rose described her future thus: *Just being stuck on t'dole, stuck in t'house.* Like Mary, Rose was in contact with a doctor, but primarily for an assortment of minor physical ailments. The last young woman to be discussed was under the care of a psychiatrist. Jane had not worked for more than a few months at a time since leaving school, and her current spell of unemployment had reached beyond four years when she was interviewed. Like Mary, Jane's problems appeared to stem from inside the family. When asked if anyone had ever made her feel useless, Jane replied:

Yes, me mum. She tells me that I am useless all the time. She has done it all my life and I don't get on with her. I've got used to it, and respond by being like I am and going to see the local psycho-therapist . . . I see a psychiatrist and get tablets. He just says that I am depressed, I suppose. I have seen five different psychiatrists and everytime there's one I like, they leave in a few weeks or I don't really get on with them. Now they are trying to find me a psycho-therapist . . . They just thought at first that I was suicidal and they wanted to put me in [institution] and then they moved — so they stopped giving me anti-depressants and now I just get sleeping tablets. And then I went to a psychiatric day-hospital but that was just useless because there wasn't anyone there, just a load of old alcoholics wandering about, so I left that. That is all they could suggest really. I don't find their medication any help. I have stopped taking it now because they wouldn't let me have anymore. *Interviewer: They say you are suicidal. Is that right?* Yes. *(Jane, London)*

Quite apart from the fact that the National Health Service appeared to have seriously failed to help this young woman, she had also been placed on probation for stealing sweets from a shop. Thus, her half-hearted attempts to find work were doomed almost before she started. Jane felt there was little she could do to change her life: the Jobcentre was not interested; her mother only nagged; she had few friends. When asked if she ever thought of marrying, she replied:

No, I don't think anyone would marry me and I don't think I will be alive long enough . . . I can't see my life changing and I know I just won't go on with it like it is . . . It is not to do with unemployment. Unemployment does make it worse.

There is very little that research such as this can say about the distress suffered by these three young women. Obviously, their problems predated entry into the labour market. However, and just as obviously, having jobs might have helped them come out of their problems by giving their lives structure and meaning. Sadly, though, it seems unlikely that any of these three will find work in a labour market that has little enough need for many young people without psychological problems, and even less need for young people with such problems.

It is probably not a coincidence that, in general, the men in this study discussed physical ill-health and the women discussed psychological ill-health, in that this difference accords with the greater willingness of women to talk about feelings, and the greater likelihood of women seeking medical help for emotional problems. However, it should be remembered that these discussions were largely spontaneous; not only does this allow the possibility that men other than Pete might have talked about similar problems if they had been asked directly, but it also allowed for many more young people, both male and female, with such problems to choose not to make reference to them in interviews. In any event, young men and women with physical or psychological health problems, or both, clearly form part of the young unemployed in our society. Under better labour market conditions, some of these young people would have found work; and some of them would have overcome their health problems. In the existing labour market, it is possible that some of them will never work and perhaps never overcome the distress and poor health which are now part of their lives without work.

In trouble; in prison
In addition to Jane above, who had been placed on probation for stealing and Daniel, in Chapter 2, who made his living illegally and thus risked prison, 4 other respondents discussed times in their lives when they had come into conflict with the authorities. These 4 — all men — had followed a rather standard route from truancy to prison, spending time on the way in approved schools and borstal. Not surprisingly, the consequences of the mistakes which had taken them to prison included prolonged spells of unemployment. As is the situation for young people with health problems, there is little room in today's labour market for young offenders. Jackie, from Manchester, described the difficulties that confront such young people at the Jobcentre:

> See, I left school the last time, like, I went down to the Job Centre, right? They said they won't give me any jobs — I don't know why . . . Like, say someone went down to the Job Centre, you know, like, some of these people who go down to the Job Centre, like, just get jobs, just like that. While some, you know, like if I went down there, like, you know, they just throw this form at me — 'fill it in here' — When I went down there, they just turned it down and that's it, you know.

Jackie suggested that he did not know the reason why he was unable to find work through the Jobcentre; however, other comments made by him in his interview very clearly revealed the source of his difficulties:

> See, I've been to a couple of schools in my life. I got expelled from two schools, right? Then they sent me up to Woodside. I nearly got ex-

pelled from there . . . See, I went to court, right, they sent me to court. I got myself into trouble, right, and then they sent me up to that scheme for about six months . . . I'm looking for a job, you know. See, I haven't had a job since I left school.

Jackie had no qualifications, no training, and no skills. Aged 20 when interviewed, he had been without work for four years.

If Jackie showed a remarkable nonchalance about his future: *Not bother me now, all I'm waiting for is to get a job, you know. The future don't bother me,* this was not the case for the following two men who had followed much the same route through life. William went from truancy to an approved school, then a spell of unemployment, a job, prison, training college, prison, another job, prison again, and had been unemployed for three years when interviewed. An unusually perceptive young man, William wanted work as a gardener. And although he knew his chances of finding such work were slim, he kept hoping:

Interviewer: Did your parents encourage you to do well at school? I never went, did I? Not the last couple of years . . . playing truant. I didn't leave school — I was stuck in the approved school . . . *Interviewer: Do you think it's important, then, for people to have jobs?* Yeah, 'cos you feel in society, like — you know you are in society. With the unemployed, you're not really in society, 'cos no one cares about you — you know, they don't really — know what I mean? Otherwise, we'd have a job . . . It's great, you know [working]. You feel as though you are in society — you feel your own person again, you know — can't explain it. Life has a sort of bit of meaning, you know, that you are doing summat and it's good to do summat . . . Just hope — that you are, you know — you are going to get a job and you are going to be successful in something, you know, you are going to have a bit of money behind you and your own house and your own car whatever — later on in life. It's to be comfortable, feel like you do — you are back in society — you're a part of society. (*William, Manchester*)

One hopes that William will find his place in society, although overcoming his prison record and current spell of prolonged unemployment will be difficult at best. At least his hopes of gardening work were more or less realistic, unlike the next young man who had much the same background as William, but who wanted the type of work which his past encounters with the police and prison system expressly prohibited. In fact, if there was ever a case of self-defeating behaviour among young offenders, Ian exemplified it:

I did okay until I was about 14 really, when I was in the primary school. I was up with the top pupils sort of thing. I went to secondary school and things just went haywire, the same old story — I mixed with the wrong people. I never touched drugs or anything like that. I used to hop off school, I started smoking, getting into trouble stealing and it just went downhill from there. When I was 16 I left school, basically I wasn't there. It started off when I used to go in and get marked in and then go. Then I never bothered at all. The crowd that I was knocking about with, we just used to do as we pleased. When I was 14 I used to work in a carpet factory — the geyser didn't want no cards or nothing — instead of going to school I used to go to the carpet factory and work there . . . They used to send letters home, and I used to get some good hidings until I was about 15, then my father said, 'It's up to you now, you go your own way', but when I got into trouble and went to borstal and that, they've never said, 'That's it, never come in this door again', they always came to see me. (*Ian, London*)

Ian followed up his time in borstal with two years unemployment, and then landed in prison. He had had a variety of short-term, unskilled jobs but his true vocation was driving — vans, lorries, whatever. But a history of offences involving cars together with licence suspensions for drink offences meant little hope of finding the work he loves:

. . . because most of the trouble that I've been in has been to do with vehicles and that, you know, ringing cars and that sort of thing. Obviously, when they punish you, they take your licence away as part of the punishment and as this is the only job that I can really get into — I get satisfaction and enjoyment out of it — they take my licence away, it's just like — it leaves me high and dry. I've tried other jobs and they just last a matter of weeks, I just sling them in because I'm either stuck in a factory or a warehouse or on a building site — I just pack it in . . . the reason why I like driving is because you go in and get your truck loaded up and you're your own boss sort of thing, so I'm happy doing that. I'm basically quite a loner sort of thing as regards work, when I'm at work, I like to be on my own — I don't like the tittle tattle that goes on in a workplace, so I do feel a lot better . . . because of that freedom. I just enjoy being out on my own sort of thing.

Ian had been out of work for almost three years when interviewed. He had little expectation of ever being employed on a long-term basis, and certainly would not find work as a driver for ten or more years:

The only thing I would really like to say is basically people who get into trouble with the law and that — they should think about, should think before they slam that endorsement on your licence which is a big punishment. That's what they did to me for drinking and driving; they slap 10 years on you, knowing that an insurance company wouldn't insure you for a company vehicle. They're just telling me that they're going to ruin my life for 10 years and that's it. Because I did explain that I love driving and that it is my living and if you do this to me, then you will be putting me on the dole for the next 2 years . . . I was never in an accident. I just got stopped. I wasn't a great deal over the limit. I knew I was when I got in the car. I accepted my ban for 2 years, fair enough. But then they said your licence will be endorsed for 10 years. That's just like banning me for 12 years, really, for my sort of employment. A lot of other people, it wouldn't affect so badly. They might be a top man in an office, so it isn't going to affect them that much.

It is hard not to feel sympathy for Ian's plight, even though he had more or less brought it on himself. The sympathy increases when one listens to Ian talk about himself:

I've always had this feeling that I've got some sort of potential somewhere; it's just waiting there for something to fall into place. I've felt that someday something is going to click and I'll be there. Although I've been in trouble, I've got quite a knack for turning my hand to things, once I get the bite of something, I go into it.

It is to be hoped that Ian gets his chance.

The last young offender to be discussed is a young British-born black of West Indian origin. In his interview Jason described a childhood of relative affluence, living in the country with his mother and sisters on a farm. When Jason was in his early teens, his widowed mother married a Black from Africa. The immediate effect of this was a clash of culture and temperament between son and husband; the far-reaching effects were Jason's entry into care, approved school and borstal. However, when living in Australia Jason was able to find employment helping other young offenders — work which allowed him to grow up and learn that this is the type of work that he wants to do. If he is unable to find similar work in Britain, Jason intends to return to Australia:

Yeah. I liked working with young offenders, kids who get in trouble with the police or just started experimenting with drugs, things like that. Because I've done a lot of stupid things — like stupid things — I've been in trouble with the police. I've been in borstal. I've done a prison sentence, I've taken drugs. I've sort of grown out of that, and I think I've got so much to offer kids who're just growing up. Usually, just catch them at the right time, they can see that if they carry on the way they're going, they're either going to end up in prison on and off for the rest of their lives, or they'll end up dead because of drugs. I feel I've got a lot to offer. And I enjoy working with them. (*Jason, London*)

119

Jason ends the review of young men and women in unemployment who have special problems, special disadvantages. As we have seen, these disadvantages cut across both ethnicity and social class, bringing into unemployment young men and women of all social classes and all skin-colours. Not all of these young people would find employment in a buoyant labour market, but most would have far better chances than is the case at present.

Notes
1. Analysis of ethnic minority groups in the 1984 survey was based upon visual classification by interviewers of respondents as being either of Asian, African, or West Indian origin. The term *black* is used as a convenient shorthand expression for respondents of Afro-Caribbean origin.

6 LIVING IN SOCIETY

Introduction

The most immediate consequences of long-term unemployment fall upon the unemployed themselves, with direct effects ensuing for household and family formation, leisure and consumption patterns, health and personal happiness. In addition, however, wider social consequences may result from large numbers of young people failing to find secure or continuous employment and, concomitantly, failing to take a full part in the surrounding society. When youth unemployment began to escalate, political and social upheaval were predicted as the most probable of these broad social consequences. However, as Hakim (1982) notes, the expected upheaval has yet to occur. Hakim outlines a number of possible explanations for the containment of high rates of unemployment within the existing social and political order. First, she suggests the possibility that our expectations about the social consequences of unemployment may be misleadingly based upon experiences of the 1930s depression, and that the elimination of absolute poverty in the 1980s through income support measures attenuates the social impact of unemployment. Secondly, she suggests that broad social consequences may in fact exist but remain largely invisible, in part because they are diffuse and widespread, and in part because we have few ways of measuring such consequences. Thirdly, she notes that the concentration of unemployment in particular regions and among particular social groups effectively prevents the spread of the social consequences of unemployment within the wider society (1982:434).

These explanations of the general absence of widespread social and political upheaval are persuasive, and should be borne in mind throughout the following analyses. However, it is the suggestions of two other writers that the present chapter intends to follow in seeking to explain the social and political perspectives of the young unemployed; to explain, that is, the ways in which young people without work accommodate living in a society where the majority of people have work. These perspec-

121

tives are assumed to be of interest in their own right; but in addition, it is hoped that an understanding of the social and political attitudes of unemployed young men and women will also lead to an understanding of their apparent acquiescence in unemployment.

Roberts (1982) concentrates on the analysis of long-term youth unemployment. He sees sub-employment — young people entering and leaving the labour force and a variety of unattractive, dead-end jobs for periods outside of formal employment — as akin to the 'cooling-out' process which occurs in North American colleges. In North America many more young people are accepted as college students than actually graduate with degrees. The high failure and drop-out rates of North American students are said to perform the latent function of lowering students' expectations and aspirations by encouraging them to accepted more limited job prospects[1]. Sub-employment, together with the tendency for young people to seek individualistic solutions to their employment problems, is suggested by Roberts as primarily responsible for young people absorbing high and persistent levels of unemployment without recourse to social or political protest.

The second writer to be drawn upon is Hugo Young. In a recent article, Young suggests that society has yet to realise the extent of change in public attitudes towards unemployment. In particular, he argues that we have come to accept unemployment as inevitable, and perhaps even desirable. He refers to Prime Minister Margaret Thatcher's thesis that *'there is no alternative . . . [that] it is ultimately for their own good that thousands upon thousands, especially in the northern cities, should be thrown out of work'* (*The Guardian*, 9 September 1986). Young makes no direct reference to the absence of social or political protest as a consequence of widespread acceptance of the inevitability of unemployment. However, if it were to be the case that the unemployed themselves held such views, then their lack of protest about the situation would be quite understandable.

These, then, are the primary themes of the present chapter: first, to determine the views that the young unemployed have about the unemployment they are experiencing or have experienced, and about their place in society, including access to consumer goods; and secondly to explore Roberts' suggestion that such young people seek individualistic solutions to their problems. And finally, to determine to what extent — if any — the young unemployed have assimilated attitudes towards unemployment which incorporate inevitability and acceptance, and which preclude taking direct action in protest. The overall objective is to address issues of wider social consequence; in doing so, however, the effects of unemployment on the individual — the immediate consequences of unemployment — must necessarily come into the discussion. Our concern is to gain an interpretative understanding of social action, and of the social situations confronting the young people interviewed; to do this, it is necessary to turn to their subjective perceptions of those situations — or, to borrow a famous phrase, to seek *the definition of the situation* offered by the young unemployed themselves.

Feeling cheated

It is sometimes suggested that unemployed young people resent their exclusion from the so-called *consuming classes.* Lack of work means lack of money; and without money, young people cannot purchase their share of consumer goods. Certainly, lack of money is a problem for the majority of the young people interviewed for this study, as was detailed in Chapter 4. However, participants were also asked if they felt cheated in any way as a result of being unemployed, in the belief that *feeling cheated* is a better measure of feeling left out of society than is wishing one simply had more money. Although questions about feeling cheated normally followed questions about money, young people were generally given the opportunity to interpret *cheated* as they chose, and the interviewers followed up that interpretation.   Somewhat surprisingly, just over half the young men, and just under half the women said that they did not feel cheated, with the most common explanation being some version of *you can only have what you earn.* Comments similar to the following were made by about half of those reporting not feeling cheated:

I had enough because I weren't earning it, I weren't entitled to it. (*Janet, Sheffield*)

You can only have what they give you, so you can't really feel cheated. (*Will, Southampton*)

No, not really. Some people wish they could have things, but that's pipe dreams . . . It's silly thinking that. When you see people with lots of things, most of them have worked hard for it. I haven't worked hard for it, I haven't been able to, so I don't begrudge them that. I know that if I had a job, I'd work hard for things that I like. (*Irene, Southampton*)

No, it's like I said before, we're all in the same boat, like. If people have money, like they have it, like, because they're working for it and they're looking for the jobs which we haven't got, like. So we're just not looking hard enough for them . . . If I haven't got it [money], I haven't got it. If I have, I spend it. (*Lee, London*)

What is interesting, of course, is that many of the young people who reported not feeling cheated, also reported missing the things that money can buy. What they did not seem to share, however, was any feeling that

123

society owed them something more than what they got through benefits. As one young man from Sheffield put it:

> It's not too bad — 'cos if you just, like if it's Pakistan you get no DHSS or owt like that, do you? So in a way this country's very — it's not too bad in a way. Least you're getting summat. (*Gerry, Sheffield*)

Not all of the young unemployed interviewed held such views, however. About one-third said they did feel cheated, and an additional 10 per cent said they felt cheated sometimes or slightly, with only minor differences in response between men and women. The inability to purchase things they wanted was the most common reason behind feeling cheated, with some resentment expressed towards friends with jobs, and hence with money to spend. Even here, though, a certain degree of passive acceptance of their position surfaced, as the words of Adam from Manchester illustrate:

> Yes, very often. You get friends and that, they say: 'Oh, I've just got this', and you think, 'mmm, well, I wouldn't have minded that'. But you just can't afford it and that's the end of it.

However, in addition to feeling cheated in terms of money, some indication of a wider sense of being cheated through being unemployed emerged. Comments such as: [other] people are coming out with a lot more than me (*Michael, London*); and when you see your parents, when they're of your age . . . they made a lot more advances than what you have (*Leroy, London*); and life, like, just seems to be passing by, like (*Ceri, Manchester*) suggest a deeper sense of resentment than simply not being able to purchase consumer goods. The fact that such comments were made by only a handful does not necessarily mean that other unemployed young people do not share these views. However, the majority were either unwilling or unable to articulate their feelings in this way. In fact, one response to feeling cheated which was expected at the outset of interviewing to be quite widespread was ultimately expressed by only a single person, a young man from Sheffield who had given up looking for work. When asked if he felt cheated in any way, he replied:

> Not because I can't buy all the things that I want, no. It's not any monetary reasons. It's just that I've been conned . . . by everybody really. You spend your life at school and they all say: 'work hard and you'll get a job, get all your results and you'll get a job'. And it's a lie . . . Nobody's personally to blame, it's everybody . . . It's a community thing, isn't it . . . builds you up and lets you down. (*Nick, Sheffield*)

It is unfortunate that this research cannot shed more light on these wider interpretations of feeling cheated. Whether this is the case because of the way the questions were phrased or because these young people were unwilling to express their views on this particular subject is unclear. Certainly one would expect a deeper level of resentment to be fairly widespread among young people who have still to be allowed full participation in society. In any event, the views which were expressed by the majority of those interviewed are not without interest. Generally, these views tend towards passive acceptance of the position in which the young unemployed find themselves. Either the young people do not feel cheated because they accept the idea that one must work for one's money — and they do not; or, they feel cheated but realise that it is simply something they must come to terms with. Moreover, it seems clear that these particular unemployed young people understand the way in which one gains access to consumer goods — through employment; and understand for whose benefit society operates — people in employment. And except for a handful who feel otherwise and express a much deeper sense of resentment, most of the young people interviewed for this study seem to accept *without rancour* their meagre financial resources and in doing so, demonstate considerable belief in the view that *you don't get owt for nowt.*

Feeling angry
It is, of course, entirely possible that young people might not feel cheated by their unemployment — might believe that you only get what you earn — and yet feel angry that they have been unable to find or keep employment. Moreover, it is difficult to imagine social upheaval occurring without anger. However, if one wishes to link the absence of social upheaval to the absence of feelings of anger among the young unemployed, differences in response between men and women immediately complicate the analysis. It is perhaps fair to suggest that rioting or other acts of aggression against society are usually perpetrated by men. However, it is also well-known that women are more likely than men to be willing to discuss their feelings. Therefore, it is difficult to know what follows from the fact that more than three-quarters of the young women asked reported that they did feel angry about being unemployed, while over half of the young men asked reported that they did not. Are most young women in fact more angry about being unemployed than young men, but not engaging in acts of social protest because they are women? Are most young men genuinely not angry about their lack of work, or do they simply refuse to discuss such feelings with an interviewer? Unfortunately, a great many of the men gave only one-word answers to questioning about feeling angry — lending some support, of course, to the suggestion that men are generally unwilling to discuss their feelings. However, not all of the men restricted themselves to a simple no:

125

Just a bit peeved. I wouldn't say angry. It doesn't bother me enough to make me angry . . . It frustrates you to a certain extent but angry, no. You've got to have something smaller to aim anger at. (*Nick, Sheffield*)

Sometimes I get annoyed at myself . . . [but] no, not at governments and things like that. That's absolutely pathetic. I mean governments can help but it's not worth getting angry. (*Brian, Sheffield*)

No *Interviewer: Why not?* Wouldn't solve anything, I suppose (*George, London*)

What is interesting about the views of these three young men is the hint they contain that these men perceived that anger directed against government, or anger about unemployment *per se*, might be futile. It takes a considerable amount of psychic energy to maintain feelings of anger against persons or things over which you have no control or which you cannot change. And for some people, *The Government* or *Unemployment* may be perceived as being too big to get angry about. In fact, the few men expressing feelings of anger, and many of the women doing so, directed their feelings at much smaller objects — most often, other people:

Yes, I think I got angry when other people put down people who were unemployed, yes . . . Well, they just generally spoke about unemployed people as if they weren't worth anything really, you know, they didn't do anything and they — things like that really. (*Ken, London*)

I get angry when I see — like when I go into a shop and there's somebody and they rabbit, rabbit to another assistant and I think I could talk ten times better than they could . . . when people don't do the job well. Then I get angry, to think that they've got a job and I haven't, because I could do that job better. (*Kate, Sheffield*)

Other objects of anger found among these unemployed young women and men include the man behind the interviewer's desk who doesn't offer you the job; the woman at the DHSS office who delays your claim; and the employer who fails to reply to your job application. Anger may need to be expressed rather than repressed, but both the manner of its expression and its object need to be thought about. Futile anger may damage the one who feels it more than it damages the recipient. And perhaps in recognition of this, almost 10 per cent of the young people in this study, when asked what advice they would give to other unemployed young people, suggested taking each day as it comes and not getting angry:

Just take each day as it comes. Don't try and rush owt, just have to take it as it comes. It's no good rushing, because if you end up rushing it'd be a waste of time and it feels worse off then. Try not to get mad, just try to keep cool, don't try and get mad at everything all the time. If you feel yourself getting mad, just ignore it, do summat else. (*Robert, Sheffield*)

What follows from these mixed responses to feeling angry found among these unemployed young people? It is possible to interpret anger against one's position in society as a feeling of denial of legitimate rights in that society. However, it is more difficult to know if a lack of anger suggests a lack of any sense of having such rights. Moreover, the young women at least were more likely than not to say that they were angry about being unemployed. Perhaps it would be more fruitful, at least momentarily, to leave aside the question of general interpretation and to turn instead to the differences in feelings of anger expressed by the young men and young women.

Speculation suggests that the anger these young women felt in the face of unemployment is a likely manifestation of the increased independence women now enjoy as a result of the changes wrought in society through the women's movement. One consequence of these changes may well be that women now have higher expectations about their lives following school, and failure to fulfill such expectations quite naturally results in anger. Observing the differing returns to education gained by these young men and women lends some support to this speculation. If the young men and women of this study who had been entirely excluded from employment up to the time of the 1984 survey are considered in isolation, then important differences with respect to returns to education in the labour market are revealed. Approximately half of the respondents in the present study (51 per cent of the men and 47 per cent of the women) had failed to secure employment of any kind prior to participating in the national survey. Concentrating first on the men, we find that in this group over half obtained no qualifications prior to leaving school, while one-quarter obtained either O- or A-levels. In contrast, almost half of the women in this group had O- or A-levels, with less than one-third being wholly unqualified. Examination of the relationship between qualifications and employment status at the time of participation in the present study shows, moreover, that more than half of the women still in unemployment when re-interviewed, but only one-quarter of the men, had O- or A-level qualifications. If these young people expected to find employment on the basis of obtaining qualifications, then the young women might well have considerably more reason for being angry about failing to do so than the men. Thus, gender differences between these unemployed young people in terms of acknowledging anger can probably be explained as partly due to differences between men and women in expressing their feelings and partly due to disappointed expectations resulting from the poorer returns to educational investment received by the women.

In addition, however, two other factors appear to underpin the differences in feeling angry found between the young men and women of this study. At different points in the interviews, participants were asked if they ever felt as if they were the only person unemployed and, further, which group or groups of people they thought were the most hard hit by unemployment. The gender differences found in response to these questions were entirely consistent with the responses to feeling angry, with the majority of men reporting that they did not feel that they were the only persons unemployed, and the majority of women reporting that they did. Overall, only one in five of the young men reported feeling isolated in this way, in contrast to one in two of the women. Moreover, 40 per cent of the women reported that they felt *both* angry *and* isolated, while, in almost perfect mirror image, virtually the same proportion of men reported that they did not feel angry and did not feel isolated. These two were the largest single groups for both men and women. Typical comments of the young people in regard to isolation were as follows:

No, not really. No, well, on an estate like this, see, there's quite a lot of it anyway, so nearly everyone knows someone. (*Archie, Southampton*)

I used to but I don't think I would now . . . my mates are on the dole now, but before everybody I know used to be working when I used to be on the dole, but its different now . . . when I were at college as well, people I know used to be working quite regularly, now they're on the dole. (*Ben, Sheffield*)

Sometimes, yeah. There's a lot of people I know who've been unemployed but now they all seem to have suddenly got jobs, and I never seem to be able to find anything. (*Jean, Sheffield*)

Yeah, at times I did because I didn't know anybody else that was unemployed. All my friends were working and all my family as well. (*Grace, Sheffield*)

Quite clearly, the success or failure in the labour market of others known to these unemployed young people — friends, neighbours, family — colours the perceptions they have of their own unemployment. It is one thing to know that there are three or four millions unemployed, and quite another to be the only one in your social world without employment. Conversely, knowing that there are others near you who are also unemployed tends to lessen feelings of isolation, although few of those asked were willing to suggest that such knowledge made unemployment any easier.

Consistent with the differences between men and women with respect to feeling isolated within unemployment were differing views about which groups in society are the most hard hit by unemployment. For the women, other young people, including school-leavers with and without qualifications, were cited most often as the hardest hit group. Nearly 40 per cent of the women mentioned young people in this regard, with no other group mentioned by more than a handful of women. In contrast, the views of the young men as to the hardest hit groups were rather evenly spread across members of ethnic minorities, people with families, and middle-aged workers — people variously aged from 30 to 55 years. Each of these three groups was mentioned by about one in five of the men, with young people referred to by only about one in ten. The contrast between the views of the men and women is clearly expressed in the following two quotations:

> You seem to want the sort of answers to say that young unemployed people are crumbling as human beings. Most of them are holding out alright. I think it affects older people who've spent their lives in work more than it does younger people. (*Michael, London*)

> More often than not it's the younger people that are hard hit by unemployment. People over 40 have been in employment, so they've made some money. But young people have no chance of making any money. That is the hardest group, the young people. There seems to be no way out, you're just going along one tunnel, and there's no exit. You're just carrying along, there's no life at the bottom of the tunnel at all. There's no jobs. And they need jobs. (*Joan, Manchester*)

In general, then, the following broad picture may be drawn of the views of these unemployed young people with respect to feeling cheated, feeling angry, and feeling isolated. First, there seems to be widespread acceptance among both men and women of the view *you only get what you earn*, and perhaps as a consequence, little apparent rancour about their inadequate financial resources. Furthermore, little evidence was found of any deeper sense of resentment assumed to be consistent with feeling cheated. Secondly, although there were important differences between men and women in feelings of anger about unemployment, with the women more likely than not to say they felt angry in contrast to the men, the anger which was expressed by both men and women was usually directed against other individuals and not against the state for failing to provide employment. Few if any of these young people, women included, demonstrate feelings of anger about their unemployment which are likely to lead to challenges to the present social order. Thirdly, the differences between the men and women with respect to feeling angered by unemployment were mirrored in their differing responses to feeling isolated within unemployment. Over half the women said that they either did feel or had felt that they were the only ones unemployed, and consistent with this, nearly half considered young people to be the hardest hit by unemployment. In contrast, 70 per cent of the young men said they did not feel they were alone in their unemployment, and their views about which groups suffered most from lack of work were more or less evenly spread across several likely groups. These gender differences warrant further comment.

Until quite recently, it was frequently assumed that unemployment affected young men more than young women, although some writers acknowledged that the frustrations of unemployment could be felt equally by both sexes (Ashton and Field, 1976). What, then, do the differences observed here signify? Are most young women in fact more angry about being unemployed than most young men? Do more young women than young men feel isolated in unemployment? It seems inadequate to suggest that gender differences either in willingness to express feelings of anger in an interview, or in returns to education account fully for the differences observed in this regard. Perhaps it is the case, then, that these young women are in truth more angry and feel more isolated in unemployment than their male counterparts.

Comparisons between men and women in the 1984 national survey certainly seem to provide ample justification for such feelings among women. In finding that it is men with the fewest social and educational advantages who tend to suffer the longest durations without work, the 1984 survey confirmed the results of previous research. Women in the 1984 survey, however, were found to be generally less socially and educationally disadvantaged in comparison with men. In other words, women in unemployment tended more often to be qualified and to have better qualifications, tended less often to come from large families, and tended less often to live in council accommodation when compared with men in the same durations of unemployment. But despite being less disadvantaged than men, women who had entered into what appears to be *chronic* unemployment — that is, women in the longest durations of unemployment measured — had had less prior success in the labour market than unemployed men with similar experiences of very long-term unemployment. Among the men and women unemployed for three years or more, 40 per cent of the women had never been employed, in contrast to 28 per cent of the men; while 61 per cent of the women either had never worked at all or had worked for only 10 per cent or less of their economically active lives, in contrast to 48 per cent of the men. The detailed analyses concerned with differing returns to education in the labour market noted earlier between the men and women in the present study who had been excluded from employment altogether are entirely consistent with this pattern of differences between men and women in the 1984 survey. For some women in unemployment, then, it seems a clear case of less for more. And for women in this study at least, feelings of anger seem to be the result.

This chapter began by remarking upon the fact that the social upheaval predicted as a consequence of widespread and prolonged youth unemployment has failed to materialise. Although it was never intended to demonstrate why the young people in this study in particular have not turned to social violence or protest, it was assumed that their views might help in understanding the more general absence of upheaval. This assumption has been borne out in the preceding analyses. These young people do not have views of their unemployment which threaten the social order of society; if anything, they are quite conservative in their views and generally accept the dominant mores of British society. As noted earlier, Roberts (1982) suggests that most young people seek individualistic solutions to their employment problems. He goes on to reason that unemployment is *one of several unpleasant facts of life to be acknowledged and accepted pragmatically rather than challenged, ideologically or politically* (1982:23). And clearly, the present study confirms this view. Feelings of anger among these unemployed young men and women, when acknowledged to exist, are most often directed at objects of psychologically manageable proportions — other people in particular. Anger against the state for not providing jobs, based upon a perceived right to work, is either missing, or seen as a waste of time. Rather than unemployment creating a pool of hostile young people desirous of overthrowing society, what it seems to be creating is an ever-larger pool of unhappy young people awaiting their turn to join society. This is not to suggest that these young people enjoy being unemployed, although at times a few do. Rather, it is to suggest that if a concerted assault on unemployment is to come from some group in society it is unlikely to come from the young unemployed. The political perspectives found among the group of young people in this study lend support to this suggestion.

Political perspectives

The attempt to understand the political perspectives of the respondents to this study was made through direct questions about their interest in political parties and organisations like the Campaign for Nuclear Disarmament, and more indirectly through questioning about why they thought there was so much unemployment and what could be done to improve matters. Analysis of the answers to these questions suggests that the gender differences apparent in the discussions of anger and isolation do not exist with respect to political attitudes. Nor do there appear to be any significant differences by geographical area. In general, like other groups of young people, the unemployed young people in this study were largely uninterested in politics per se, with approximately two-thirds of both men and women reporting that they had no interest either in the main political parties or in organisations such as CND[2]. About half of both sexes responded to these direct questions with equally direct one-word answers. Of the half offering views beyond a simple yes or no, however, one-third expressed the belief either that political parties were all the same once in government or that none of them was any good, whether in government or not. A further third expressed support for the Labour Party, although this support was often accompanied by doubt about Labour's ability to remedy the unemployment situation. Only a handful spoke favourably of the Conservative Government. Sometimes considerable disgust with the political parties surfaced, as expressed in the following:

> I think that they're all corrupt, self-centred and they just work public opinion to their advantage. They do not actually work in — they're not working the revolutions to their advantage and then getting public opinion. They work public opinion by what they are going to do, not what they have done, and they never do what they are going to do. (*Brian, Sheffield*)

> Yes, they're all the bloody same. They all go on the tele. We this and we that — we do this. They do sod all when they get in there. They're all like Mrs. Thatcher — done-bugger all when she got in there. And she made all the promises God created. It's all talk. And they're all the ruddy same — all Parliament. You know, they're all for themselves, quite honestly. (*Christopher, Southampton*)

But even when disgust was absent, the belief that there is little to choose between the parties remained:

> Well, quite honestly, I don't know where I am with them. Because I mean, you see that much news about them and they all appear to be doing badly. I mean, I can't say I would choose Mrs. Thatcher. I admire her — she sticks to it, but she doesn't do a lot for anybody, except people like herself, the more wealthy, hoping to be more wealthy. (*Andrew, Sheffield*)

> Well, they're all the same really. As far as I've ever seen that any government has affected, you know, normal life. They're much the same. Everything goes up every year. It's all the same really. Nothing's really changed a lot. (*Archie, Southampton*)

Quite clearly, these young people are not without political attitudes even though they report lack of interest in political parties. This fact became particularly apparent through analysing their responses to questioning about why unemployment is so widespread. Paramount among the explanations offered was Mrs Thatcher and the policies of the Conservative Government, with this response coming from over one-third of the young men and women. However, next in frequency among the explanations offered were views which Mrs. Thatcher herself might willingly accept. As noted at the outset of this paper, Hugo Young has suggested that we have yet to realise the extent of the change in public attitudes and the level of acceptance of the inevitability of unemployment, arguing that the views of the Conservative Party have been successfully promulgated since 1979. It should be remembered that the oldest of the young people in the study were only 27 years old, and that the Conservatives are therefore the only government known to the majority. Hence, it should not be too surprising that many of these unemployed young people had assimilated the arguments of the Conservative Party regarding the causes of unemployment. The following comments are typical of approximately one-fifth of the respondents offering opinions about the causes of unemployment:

> Save you win contracts, you're not going to get more jobs. You can't win contracts on the wages you're on. And nobody's going to take a pay cut, why should they? Like I say, you've got to start from the bottom, haven't you? You've got to win orders — less pay, but that's not on the individual person — that's the whole country that's got to do that. (*Thomas, Manchester*)

> I think everybody's got to work and they've got to get orders from abroad again. It's like I said, other countries have lost faith in us through strikes and that. We've got to build up their faith again to get, you know, exports. (*Grace, Sheffield*)

> People have been so used to being employed by big companies and now perhaps we are going back the other way. People should perhaps learn to employ themselves . . . I think people have been so used to having a job that is ready for them . . . (*Sarah, London*)

> You can't blame it all on the government because it's worldwide . . . [but] I think that the firms have a lot to do with wanting bigger wages. If they didn't have such big wages, firms could afford to sell things cheaper and people could afford to buy them. In the end, people would be made — more people would be in employment than unemployed. I think really the employers who've had to put wages up because people wanted more money, so of course goods have had to go up and prices have had to go up and it ends up in one vicious circle, no one can afford

to buy them, so the firm goes bust. That's my opinion. (*Adam, Manchester*)

If there's more jobs, there is going to be more inflation. I hope that it [unemployment] doesn't improve. (*Janet, Sheffield*)

The last comment was made by a young woman who was in work when interviewed, having experienced only one spell of unemployment which lasted about one year. This young woman is not typical of the others sharing these views, however, in that all but a few were unemployed when interviewed and had been for an average of two to three years. Other comments along these same lines included the belief that too many imports were causing unemployment; wages were too high; unemployment was keeping wages down; and that cuts in rates and taxes could improve the job situation.

It should, perhaps, be reiterated that the unemployed young men and women holding these views represented only about 20 per cent of those offering explanations for unemployment, and that an equal proportion held no views at all on this issue. Nevertheless, it is interesting to discover that such perspectives on unemployment exist among the young unemployed, to whatever extent. In addition to the views noted above, a further small group of men and women believed that the unemployed were themselves to blame for unemployment, by virtue of not looking hard enough for work:

I don't know, I'm well — I think there's quite a few people that are unemployed that just don't give a damn — they don't even bother looking for work. They think, 'well, why should I go out and work when I can get it for nothing' . . . I don't really know, I just don't understand. I mean, I know there's lots of jobs if you go out and really look for them, but sometimes people just don't look in the right places . . . (*Jenny, Manchester*)

I think some people don't want to work. I think a certain percentage of the unemployed don't want to work . . . (*Ken, London*)

The jobs are there but people are not looking for them . . . probably because if they've been out of work for a long time, they get into a rut and the habit of not having a job (*Stephanie, London*)

Does it follow from this that unemployment has come to be accepted as inevitable by these unemployed young men and women? If it is possible to interpret the belief that unemployment can be reduced as disproving belief in its inevitability, then, for the men at least, the answer is a clear no. Nearly three-quarters of the men asked if unemployment could be reduced responded affirmatively; less than 10 per cent thought nothing could be done to improve the situation. The women, however, were much less sure that unemployment could be improved, with barely half responding affirmatively and nearly 40 per cent reporting that they did not know. Superficially at least, the views of the women in this regard seem consistent with their feelings of anger and isolation as described earlier. In addition, the differences between the men and women here are consistent with the finding that slightly more women than men see the future in general as getting worse and slightly fewer women than men see their own futures as getting better.

However, even allowing for these apparent differences between men and women, the majority did believe that things could be done to improve unemployment, hence it would be difficult to argue that they see joblessness as inevitable. But if unemployment is generally not accepted as inevitable, what might be the likely political responses of these unemployed young people? Or, are there likely to be any political responses to unemployment from this group? As discussed, the level of political involvement of the majority is minimal. Sixty-five per cent of both men and women were found to have little or no interest in politics, either of the conventional kind or in alternative groups such as CND. About half expressed no political opinions of any kind, responding to interviewers' questions with a simple yes or no. Of those expressing opinions, about one-third saw little to choose between the main political parties, and were therefore unlikely to agitate for conventional political change. Another third tended to support the Labour Party, but often this support was tinged with considerable doubt about the Labour's ability to do anything about unemployment. And finally, there was the small but not insignificant group who tended to accept the prevailing explanations of the causes of unemployment embodied by Mrs Thatcher's *there is no alternative.* This group is perhaps especially unlikely to engage in political activity to change the status quo. It seems doubtful, then, that unemployed young people such as those studied here will prove to be likely recruits for political agitation or change. Nevertheless they generally believe that the government should be doing more to remedy unemployment, with over 70 per cent of both men and women suggesting that it could and should act to lessen unemployment. The solutions they offer for improving the job situation are ones which have long been discussed in the public realm and include spending more money on education and the health service and on the infrastructure of the country; creating training schemes for older as well as younger workers; lowering the retirement age; and creating additional job-splitting or job-sharing schemes. It should be emphasised that these young people were not asked for their views on how to solve the problem of unemployment in the expectation that new or unique solutions would thus appear. Nor was it intended that the victims of unemployment should be held responsible for curing unemployment. Rather, the intention was to discover what actions — if any — these young unemployed perceived as being possible solutions. And what appears to be largely missing from their solutions, perhaps with good reason, is any suggestion that individual action through protesting against unemployment could be effectively undertaken in order to overcome widespread joblessness.

Participants were asked if they thought that people, including themselves, should protest against unemployment, and if so, in what ways. No gender differences surfaced in response to the first part of this questioning, with about one-third of both men and women suggesting that people should protest; one-quarter arguing that people did protest already but it did no good, and one-quarter uncertain or against protest. The belief that protesting is likely to be futile appears to be based on the view that no one notices the unemployed very much anymore; that they — the unemployed — have become rather a forgotten group in society:

> I think people have got used to it now. People have got used to the fact that there are so many people unemployed and people listening to the news just don't take it in any more. (*Marcia, Southampton*)

> Nobody seems to want to talk about unemployment somehow. That gets me annoyed . . . they don't seem bothered. (*Vincent, Sheffield*)

But in addition, the government is viewed as unlikely to listen to the protests of unemployed people:

> I don't think [protest helps] because they [the government] wouldn't take any notice anyway. They'd just put it down to 'Oh, it's all them lot that can't get jobs or that don't want to work, just ignore them' (*Jean, Sheffield*)

> I don't think any protest would — the people who really matter would just mock them, because they're all right . . . (*Daniel, Sheffield*)

And despite the fact that nearly 60 per cent of these young men and women believe that people should protest against unemployment, whether or not it is effective, very few indeed had any concrete ideas about how to protest. Over half had no opinions at all about the ways in which people, or they themselves, might take action against unemployment. A scattering of individuals felt that writing to MPs would possibly be effective, another scattering felt that petitions might help. Only one group of any interest surfaced among the few who did offer concrete suggestions — about one-quarter of the men who argued for collective responses to the problems of the unemployed:

Oh, definitely. We ought to get an organised leadership, sort of thing, I should think. And proper ways of putting things forward. There probably is already. There's an action centre for unemployment [in town] but I don't really know much about it . . . I think the unemployed should just become a bit more organised together. I don't think the government would like us to become organised. (*John, Sheffield*)

Well, for every individual, you know, as an individual, I don't see what people really can do. I mean, you know, you've got to form a group and then go to some higher power to try and do something about it . . . but, you know, with government policies like they are today, I myself can never see unemployment drop, never. (*Bernie, Southampton*)

It would be good, definitely. I think that if in one family there was one person unemployed, the people who were working should do something on their behalf, like go on strike at work. Things like that. (*Colin, Manchester*)

None of these men had themselves ever engaged in collective protest, however. If concrete suggestions about ways of protesting were missing from the responses of many of these young people, so too were demands for violent forms of protest. The inner city riots of the 1980s were discussed with 7 male respondents of West Indian origin living in London[3]. The views of these 7 young men about the riots were quite mixed, although they all agreed that the social situations in which ethnic minorities find themselves in inner cities and in Britain generally are far more important to any explanation of social unrest than is unemployment *per se*. Nevertheless, 4 of these men saw linkages between the riots and unemployment. The other 3 denied such links, 2 because they personally knew employed young men who had taken part in recent disturbances. The third man had never really thought much about the issue, but felt that rioting was unlikely to be connected to unemployment. Only 2 of these 7 men thought violent protest was any good, and the views of these 2 were virtually unique in the present research.

Perhaps it is not too surprising that the young unemployed of this study seem unlikely to question or challenge the existing social order. Visualising that life could be different, inventing alternative social worlds and the ways to achieve those different worlds, takes a considerable amount of creativity. These young men and women have few educational resources. They have little access to the ways of thinking available to would-be social reformers. Rather than wishing to overthrow society, the young people of this study would much rather get jobs and join society.

The future

If it is true that most of the young unemployed of this study are in fact

137

waiting to join rather than to overthrow society, how then do they see their future chances? What do they believe the future holds, not just in general but for themselves personally? Previous research would have us believe that such young people see no future for themselves, or see only misery and hardship. Cashmore, for example, describes modern youth as anticipating future lives which are *impoverished, precarious, narrow and restrictive* (1984:6); while Coffield and his colleagues paint a similarly bleak picture of youth in the 1980s:

> Since the last war, the young have never had it so bad . . . Their flat pessimism extended to all futures, personal, national and global, but they rarely let it affect their lives from day to day. (1986:1)

The present research suggests, however, that the expectations which unemployed young people have of the future do not lend themselves to such straightforward and pessimistic categorisation. In this study are young men and women who, realistically or not, see their personal futures as relatively bright, whatever happens in society as a whole. In addition, there are young men and women who believe that nothing the future holds for them can be in any way as bad as the present, and they too see better prospects ahead. In many respects, these young people may just be suffering from the optimism said to be natural to the young and thus be heading for considerable disappointment, but such young men and women are nonetheless part of the young unemployed. There are, of course, young men and women in this study who, like those interviewed by Cashmore and Coffield, see no future, either for themselves or for Britain generally. For them, unemployment has taken its toll. However, what is important to note is that young people without work are not a homogeneous mass. This has been demonstrated throughout this research, and it is reaffirmed through the views young men and women hold of their futures in society which consist of many strands and varying degrees of both optimism and pessimism. It is not all bleak.

Part of the investigation into the views these young unemployed men and women have of their futures concentrated upon their expectations for society in general: did they see unemployment improving or getting worse over the years? In response to this questioning, there was near unanimity between the sexes, with approximately 80 per cent of both men and women suggesting that the future would either get worse or remain the same — which was bad enough. Slightly more women than men felt that the job situation would remain stable rather than worsen. Only a handful of men, and fewer women, suggested that unemployment would improve in the future; while another small group suggested that it would have to get worse before it got better:

I think it's going to get a lot worse and then it might get a little — yes, it will improve actually, but not before it gets worse. And it'll never get back to the sixties — you know, when you could pick and choose a job any time like — it's never going to get back to that. (*Brian, Sheffield*)

It's got to get worse, to get better. I'm a firm believer in that. It's got to really hit rock bottom before anyone's going to actually realise, because now it's just a stalemate. I think people just accept that this is the way: 'We've got three million unemployed — so what?' That's it. Whereas if it really hits an all-time low, then they've got to pull their finger out and think: 'My God!' — and then they've got to do something. (*Kate, Sheffield*)

It is going to take a long time for it to get back on its feet. I think it might get worse. No one thought it would get worse four years ago. It wouldn't surprise me if it got worse now. (*Kathy, Manchester*)

I think it's going to get worse. I think it's going to be 6 or 7 million. (*Helen, Manchester*)

I think it might get a bit better but I don't think it will ever get back to being fully — to everyone being back in work. I think there'll always be a percentage of unemployed but I think it will get better gradually, but it won't happen that quickly, I don't think. (*Ken, London*)

It is interesting to compare the near unanimity among these unemployed young men and women about the improbability of the unemployment situation improving with their similar agreement that the government should — and could — take action to create more jobs. Quite clearly, these young people think that government action is *possible but not probable*. However, a more important comparison is with the views they hold about their personal futures. For although only a very few think that unemployment in general will improve, many more believe that their own lives will get better. Just over half of the men and almost 40 per cent of the women were looking forward to better futures:

I don't think it can get much worse. Overall it has got to get better. But for me it is, for me personally, it's getting better. And if the rest of the country can jump on me back and keep going with me — I think it's got to come for the better. (*Patrick, Sheffield*)

When I'm 30? Hopefully riding about in a posh car, having money. No, I'd just like to be a bit more independent. If I can't get a job, then I think the best thing is to start on my own, it's easier said than done. I think if you strive for things it eventually will come your way . . . I think you should never think that things are never going to change. I think things do change and you don't always realise it straight away —

sometimes a lot later on you think back and realise that they've changed — I think for the better, really. (*Sue, Manchester*)

Optimistic. I'm planning on a course this year actually, building management. If I succeed with that I think I'd do well ... I'm not planning on getting a job, I'm planning on going on further on my own, advertise for work meself. I don't like working for people anyway, if you see what I mean. I prefer to be me own boss, so that's something I'll try out. (*Frank, London*)

Only the young man above from Sheffield was in work when interviewed, and his job was due to end within six months. Nonetheless, these three and others like them believed — or at least hoped — that their futures would be bright. In fact, being in or out of work at interviews made only a slight difference to the level of optimism expressed by these young men and women.

However, it is important not to overstate the extent to which the young unemployed of this study held optimistic views of the future. About one in ten refused to consider the future at all, preferring to live one day at a time. In addition, young men and women who were looking forward to nothing — neither work nor families nor homes of their own — were well-represented. For them, perhaps the most frustrating aspect of unemployment is that it renders looking forward futile. Unemployment, and the threat of unemployment, means that plans made in hope come to nothing:

You can't really say. You got a job, and you make plans to buy a house or summat or a car. Save up for about three years, save up for a car, and about a year later, you're made redundant or you get sacked or something and then that's gone down the drain ... I don't look forward to nowt like. I just take it as it comes. You can't really plan too far ahead. Be a waste of time in some cases. You just might be lucky and it might work out for you, but you might not. Best to take each day as it comes. (*Robert, Sheffield*)

Everytime I make plans something goes wrong, so I don't bother now — like save up £15 a week. I did a right big plan, how much I would have at so many years and I lost my job, first job, so I thought 'Oh well'. Then I did the same a couple of weeks ago and then me mother says 'You're out in four weeks', so I screwed that up and so now I just don't make plans. (*Janet, Sheffield*)

What plan can you make? You can't make a lot of plans unemployed. (*Adam, Manchester*)

Quite clearly, the lack of secure employment, or of any employment at all, puts young people at the mercy of events to a much greater extent than is the case for men and women in work; with this comes loss of control over the future. And without control, why make plans?

In this study, then, both optimism and pessimism about the future are found. Many of the young unemployed would sum up their future prospects with a single word: *bleak*. Many others, though, look forward with hope, for them life cannot really get any worse, it can only improve. But however optimistic many of these young men and women are, they nonetheless expect to be out of work in the future, often on more than one occasion; and the majority foresee money becoming more difficult the longer they are without work. Few expect to own their own homes or cars, with only one in three of both men and women suggesting that this could happen. Just over 10 per cent of the women, but none of the men, suggested that home ownership would come with marriage; and in the light of the evidence presented in Chapter 4 about marriage on the dole, the expectations of these women are quite likely to be fulfilled. For the others, however, the penalty of being young in an uncertain labour market may mean prolonged exclusion from the kind of goods that only money can buy.

It may be thought that the emphasis in this section has been placed too much on the optimism some of the young unemployed feel for their futures and too little on the grim reality of youth unemployment. In part this emphasis has come from the views expressed by the young men and women themselves when discussing the future. But, in addition, the changes wrought in the moods and lives of many of these young people once they obtained employment and escaped from unemployment (however temporarily) reinforces optimism. Virtually all the men and women interviewed considered that being unemployed changed them personally, and usually for the worse. Once in jobs, though, these changes in mood, in spirit, were themselves changed — but now for the better. The words of the following young man and young woman illustrate the resilience of youth:

> Well, I'm hoping to get a high position at work eventually. I'd like to be married one day and have a family. I don't think I could ever be as badly off as I was when I was unemployed. So I think that even if — there's bound to be problems in the future but I can't see myself as badly off as I was. (*Grace, Sheffield*)

> *Interviewer: Did being unemployed change you?* Just temporarily, yeh. You're not easy to get on with any more. It's just a worrying sort of aspect of it, changing you. But once you get a job or training or whatever, that's all water under the bridge. (*Aziz, Manchester*)

Clearly, many of this generation of young people are not yet perma-

141

nently scarred by joblessness, and may not forever miss out on the satisfactions and rewards employment can bring. Moreover, it is to be hoped that the others in this research who have not yet been fortunate enough to find work still have age on their side, and they too will some-day come out of their prolonged stay in unemployment. Such was the expectation of the following young man. For the sake of the rest, let us all hope he is correct:

> It may do, 'cos as you get older you've got more chance. They're not employing younger people, they want older people [so] I may get a decent job one day. (*Dennis, London*)

Notes
1. For an early discussion of 'cooling-out' see Clark, 1960.
2. This finding contrasts rather markedly with the work done by Coffield and his associates who report that 'the young adults confessed that this [the nuclear issue] was one of their major concerns' (1986:193). However, as David Marsland (*Sociology*, November 1986) points out in a review of Coffield's work, scarcely more than a page and a half is sub-sequently devoted to the topic of nuclear issues in the book. The present study found only rare instances of concern about nuclear arms or the use of nuclear energy.
3. The original intention was to discuss the inner city riots with all respondents. However, the author was advised very strongly that such discussion was inherently racist, and invited racist comments from respondents. Thus, somewhat against her judgement, but on the advice of others more conversant with the field of ethnic relations, only black respondents were questioned on this issue.

7 IN CONCLUSION

The aim of this study has been to document the social and personal experiences of young men and women in long-term unemployment. Insofar as this aim has been successful, the study has revealed the diversity of response to prolonged joblessness. With other studies, then, this report confirms that there is no single way that young people confront life without work; rather, such young people bring to the experience of unemployment their past successes and failures in school and in the labour market, and their differing hopes and expectations for the future. But despite this diversity, some general conclusions, and their policy implications, may be drawn. The present chapter sets out these general conclusions.

First, however, a few words are needed about the group of young people selected for study. Although originally drawn from a randomly-selected national study of young men and women in long-term unemployment, the men and women studied here do not themselves constitute a representative sample of the young unemployed nor do they encompass all possible cases of youth unemployment. This is a study of the experiences of 119 young men and women living in selected areas of Britain in 1986. But if the study does not describe all experiences of unemployment among young people, the previous chapters have demonstrated that it includes a wide range of such experiences. Therefore, although it is not possible from this study to conclude with certainty that this or that proportion of unemployed young people exhibits this or that response to unemployment, it is possible through these 119 young men and women to see broad strands of experience and response which, given similar young people in similar circumstances, are likely to exist on a wider scale.

Getting jobs
Perhaps the most striking — and most important — finding to emerge from this study is the importance the majority of these young men and women place on having jobs. This was demonstrated by their continued

search for employment in the face of repeated failure and disappointment, and in their willingness to stay in jobs which were poorly-paid or otherwise unattractive just to avoid further unemployment. Only 5 men and one woman reported that they had given up looking for work altogether at the time of interview. More than three-quarters stated that they continued to visit Jobcentres in their search for work despite the fact that there were rarely suitable jobs there and despite feeling that the jobs available through the public service tended to be of poor quality. In interview after interview, the advice these young people offered themselves, and others like them, was to *keep looking; don't give up*.

To some people, this finding may be surprising. In the first place, it goes against caricatures of the young unemployed which picture them as work-shy dole scroungers. Secondly — and more substantially — it exists within ever-lengthening durations of joblessness. Among the men of this study, one in two had been in his current spell of unemployment for three or more years when interviewed; one in five for five or more years. And although fewer women than men remained in unemployment at the time of interview, those who were without jobs had been so for durations comparable to the men. In studying young people experiencing such prolonged joblessness, it would not have been surprising to find that their desire for work had disappeared. In the event, however, the opposite was found to be true. There appeared, moreover, to be two main influences behind the continuing importance these young people attach to finding work. First, the young men and women of this study are inevitably getting older. The youngest were about age 20 when interviewed; the oldest about age 27. These are the ages when having a home and family of one's own becomes attractive, when doing nothing loses any appeal it may once have had. Not having secure employment — or any employment at all — clearly hinders the movement of young people towards residential and financial independence. Attendant upon this is the sense that life is somehow passing by, moving too quickly, without any personal progress being made. Jobs provide the vehicle whereby young people gain their own places in society and thus, for these young people jobs remain important.

Secondly, as years spent without work pass and these young men and women get older, more and more school-leavers join the labour market. The threat posed by school-leavers to their chances of employment was discussed in interviews by young men and women who feel that today's school-leavers may well be more attractive to employers by virtue of being younger, better trained, and without histories of prolonged unemployment. The two-year Youth Training Scheme in particular was mentioned as providing opportunities for school-leavers which were not available to their own generation of young people. In combination, these two influences give substance to the general feeling found among many of these young people that theirs is the generation which has somehow been left behind, misled, or has missed out. In combination, they give a sense of urgency to the importance attached to having jobs.

The implications of this are clear. While these young men and women continue to want employment and if they are not to become a permanent underclass in society — unemployed and unemployable — action will need to be taken to reintegrate them into the labour force. The majority have only limited work experience. Economic recovery alone, even if it does generate new jobs, will not necessarily bring them into the labour force, as employers seek out workers with better experience and without the stigma of prolonged joblessness. Permanent unemployment is a real danger. Although the long-term unemployed of the 1930s were soon re-absorbed into employment with the advent of war and economic recovery, the long-term unemployed of the 1980s face a substantially more difficult task in finding work. Productivity in Britain has been increasing in recent years despite falling employment. A smaller labour force, in other words, is producing more. Moreover, the jobs many of the young unemployed are presently able to do are precisely the jobs that have disappeared. Thus, permanent unemployment, if it comes, may be no more than the result of being caught in a historical transition, as Britain sheds the last of its outdated manufacturing and enters the new-technology world of the twenty-first century. Hence, it is rarely the fault of the individual young men and women in the study and others like them that they have not moved into employment. Rather, they are victims of deep social and economic changes within our society which are restructuring not only the labour market itself but ways of entry into the labour market through education and training. The young unemployed of this study generally recognize that they are victims. At the rational level, they rarely blame themselves for their own unemployment, although they often suffer feelings of failure and inadequacy. Solving their dilemma, however, requires more than simply understanding its causes.

If, therefore, many members of this generation of young people are not to be consigned permanently to unemployment, substantial efforts will have to be undertaken to get them into permanent jobs. Moreover, these efforts will largely need to be undertaken at the societal level, through government initiative. In addition to government-led initiatives designed to encourage employers to recuit the long-term unemployed, however, measures directed at improving individual employability are also likely to be necessary. The findings of the present study make it clear that many unemployed young people are in need of better advice and counselling about the opportunities which currently exist. This was seen particularly in reference to training opportunities. A substantial number of the young men and women interviewed had lost (or never acquired) belief in the value of training or skills upgrading. Thus, there is not only a need for training programmes which will overcome any existent educational or skill deficiences among these and similar unemployed young people, but also a need for the creation of effective means of convincing such young people about the value of training. Two recent government initiatives hold out the possibility of these needs being met.

The first was the creation of a system of Job Clubs in late 1986. Job Clubs are intended to improve the employment chances of the long-term unemployed through improving the ways in which work is sought. Help and advice is given to the unemployed person with respect to job search, interviews, and presentation of self. The second initiative, begun in early 1987, is the Job Training Scheme (JTS). Although somewhat controversial in design, JTS intends to help the long-term unemployed take stock of their existing skills, review their potential for further training, equip them with better knowledge of how to obtain and retain employment, and provide an opportunity to gain established vocational qualifications. JTS will provide workplace training, and is designed to help over 100,000 trainees. At the time of writing, neither of these initiatives had been in place long enough for evaluations of their effectiveness to be undertaken. It is hoped that the intended aims of each will be fulfilled, and that effective ways of assisting the generation studied in this report into stable employment thus found. However, the findings of the present study suggest that the aims of JTS may well be difficult to fulfil, at least with respect to the generation studied here. It was clear from their interviews that many of the young unemployed did not think highly of the government schemes they had already experienced. Others felt they had missed out because the scheme they participated in, primarily the Youth Opportunities Programme, became better with its replacement by the Youth Training Scheme after their participation had ended. These feelings are unlikely to predispose them favourably towards JTS, and there is the danger that by the time JTS is improved, they will once again have moved on and thus missed out.

Living without work
An overriding objective of this study has been to understand just what life is like for unemployed young men and women. Sometimes, young people's lives on the dole are caricatured as not so bad: after all, they are young, they don't really mind doing nothing, having lots of leisure time, they don't really need that much money and so on. Or, alternatively, young people without work are portrayed as harbingers of some new work-free world, creating alternative life-styles based upon freedom from the demands of the work ethic. The reality of living on the dole is, of course, quite different.

146

It is clear from the study that the majority of these unemployed young men and women want lives which differ little from the lives of people in work: they want homes of their own, children, cars, and a little money to fall back on when needed. They would like to take a holiday now and again, and buy more of the things they see in shops. All of these require money, however; and, as these young, jobless men and women understand all too well, money comes from jobs. Without jobs, the lives they lead are only pale imitations of the lives they see others enjoying. They stay at home more often than other *employed* young people; they have fewer possessions; they have fewer options.

In large measure, the restrictions on their lives are imposed by lack of money. But having an inadequate income is not the only consequence of joblessness for young people without work. Having a job provides a structure to the day and a sense of rhythm to the weeks and months of each year. Without jobs, young people are forced to confront daily the task of finding something to do — something that gives meaning to their lives. For most of us, this is such a daunting task that it is not surprising that being bored epitomises being unemployed. For young people without work, however, this boredom may perhaps be more disturbing than for older unemployed men and women. The young people of this study are at the stage when they should be getting on with their lives. Instead, these unemployed young men and women are only getting by, just surviving. They live the same life as the rest of us, they just live less of it.

Getting married

In Chapter 4 the social relationships of the unemployed young men and women in the study were documented. Here it was seen that, for the majority, friendships exist and persist despite unemployment, and that relations with parents, although often troubled, are rarely broken altogether. In these aspects of living on the dole, life does go on, even if that life is rather unsatisfactory and certainly less than it would be with employment. However, in one area of life the effects of unemployment were seen to be quite marked. Almost one-third of both young men and women studied reported that they did not wish to marry. Furthermore, almost two-thirds of the men said they would not marry if unemployed. For the majority of women who did wish to marry eventually, however, the employment of their future husbands outweighed their own employment in importance.

It is always difficult to know how much weight should be attached to answers to hypothetical questions, and it is always possible that the young men (in particular) and young women of this study will marry someday despite saying now that they do not wish to and despite remaining unemployed. These two caveats notwithstanding, the findings of the study suggest marked consequences flowing from unemployment with respect to marriage intentions. Certainly, among many young people a dislike of marriage in general was apparent. For many of the men, this general dislike was overlaid by reluctance to marry without employment. For many of these men, moreover, such reluctance was grounded in the reality of their current rejection by young women as a result of their persistent joblessness. Young men with three, four, and five years of unemployment behind them, and unknown years ahead of them, have little to offer future marriage partners — or, at least, so it appears to the young men themselves and to some young women.

In addition to not wishing to marry if unemployed, an overwhelming majority of the men stated that they would not have children without first finding work. As with marriage on the dole, the views of the women about having children if unemployed tended to be conditional more upon the employment status of their future husbands than upon their own employment. Rather surprisingly, however, fewer women than men reported wanting children someday, when asked about this issue independently of employment status. Of course, the same caveats hold with respect to having children as about marriage intentions. Nonetheless, it seems clear that unemployment has direct consequences for the future family plans of many of these young people, and in particular for the future plans of the young men. Moreover, in the light of the findings of this study about the differing economic circumstances of unemployed married men and unemployed married women, as documented in Chapter 4, the young men appear to have good grounds for their reluctance to marry and have children while without work.

It is possible, then, that not only are many of these young people in danger of being excluded more or less permanently from the world of employment unless remedial action is taken, but many may find themselves without the pleasures and support which family life can bring. It should be remembered that these young people are at the age when marriage and children become attractive. They are, in other words, no longer teenagers. At their ages, it should be their time to marry, to have children, to create homes. But such plans are felt to be impossible; as being something others do, something *employed* people do, and not for them.

Futures without work?
One of the more important foci of this study has been the attempt to understand the social and political responses of these young men and women to long-term joblessness. Accordingly, questions about feeling cheated and feeling angry, and about protesting against unemployment were raised. However, as Chapter 6 documents, the results of this line of questioning were mixed and somewhat inconclusive. With respect to feel-

ing cheated, the young men and women were almost equally divided between those who did feel cheated and those who did not. In contrast, over three-quarters of the women reported feeling angry about their unemployment, while over half of the men reported not feeling angry. Over half of both men and women, however, felt that people should protest against unemployment, although few were certain what form such protest should take. Underlying these diverse responses were explanations which ranged from *you don't get owt for nowt* and *it's all a waste of time* to suggestions that the unemployed should form organised protest groups.

When interviewed, then, the unemployed young people of this study were as divided in their social and political responses to unemployment as they were regarding other areas of life on the dole. Perhaps the clearest finding to emerge from this aspect of the study is that, so far at least, few of the young unemployed are likely to pose a direct threat to the present social and political order of society (cf. Dahrendorf, 1987). It is the case, however, that evaluation of their social and political responses is somewhat uncertain owing to the special situation in which such young people find themselves. The question which arises with respect to evaluation is, to what other group in society should unemployed young men and women be compared? Although many of the unemployed come from similar social class backgrounds, they themselves do not constitute a social class. Nor are they an interest group in any sense that this term is normally used. And although they may appear to others as The Unemployed, to themselves they are simply unemployed at present. As the study demonstrates, many of these young people expect to be in work in the future (however temporarily); they expect, moreover, their futures to be better than their presents and their pasts. For these young people, unemployment is not seen as a permanent state, but rather as a temporary condition to be tolerated, endured, and overcome (cf. Daniel, 1981).

Moreover, it is possible that the belief that unemployment is a transitory state provides the key to understanding the diversity of their social and political responses and their apparent compliance with the condition of unemployment. If unemployment is something that will, sooner or later, be replaced by employment, then there is little cause to see oneself as part of a collectivity or class, capable of collective or class action. Moreover, as these young people look forward to ending their unemployment, it is to their future identities in society that they look, as workers of various kinds, as fathers or mothers. Being unemployed is something which is happening to them now, but not something upon which they wish to build identities.

Further, in order to take united action, the unemployed — or some part of the unemployed — must, at the least, see themselves as united in circumstance, as having common cause with other unemployed men and women. But at present, for most of the young people of this study, unemployment is seen as an individual problem. Joblessness may not be the fault of any one individual, but it is nonetheless up to that individual to seek his or her own solution to unemployment, and develop his or her own strategies for coping with it. Moreover, at present, individual solutions can still bring individual success.

However, one important aspect of this study was to document the extent to which unemployment appeared to be a more or less permanent state for many of the young men and women interviewed. It is difficult indeed to see four or five years of unemployment as transitory, however optimistic one may be. Furthermore, in the absence of concerted remedial action, it is likely that some number of those currently experiencing five years without work will go on to experience joblessness for ten, fifteen, or twenty years. If this does occur, then collective responses arising from collective awareness are possible. It is, in fact, more than possible to imagine the development of a *matured unemployed underclass* — a class of men and women, smaller in number than at present but older in years, finding common cause in the fact that they, and they alone, have been left out of the mainstream of society. Unemployed, and by then, unemployable, such a class could all too easily become ripe for orchestration in civil disorder or extremist protest if other social conditions were favourable, especially with the emergence of effective leadership.

However, the majority of the young unemployed will have been socialised to compliance, and in any event, they are hardly revolutionary material (cf. Dahrendorf, 1987). Thus, it is also possible that men and women experiencing more or less permanent exclusion from employment will never develop any sense of common identity, or in the face of common identity, lack the power or means to take collective action. In this, perhaps more probable situation, men and women without work would continue to take upon themselves individual responsibility for their dilemma of unemployment. And, lacking the resources to do much more than survive, form a permanent mass of disaffected, alienated onlookers, with little else to do but watch the rest of society getting on with their lives. Such people would, no doubt, become progressively less visible to the rest of society. Their talents would be wasted; their lives lost. Left behind through little fault of their own, these men and women would gradually just fade away. Neither prospect is pleasant, and both offend the goals that all political parties in Britain have set themselves in the post-war period.

Policy implications

The unemployed young men and women of this study have one major advantage — they are young. Therefore, there is still time for them to escape or be rescued from their joblessness and become full members of society. The resilience such young people show when finally employed was discussed in Chapter 6. But in order to be resilient, they do need jobs. If this study were about older workers confronting the possibility of permanent unemployment — too young to be retired but not wanted in the labour force — the solutions available would be different, and would focus on social remedies. For these young people, however, the only solutions which would be more than palliative are labour market solutions. For these young people, there is little alternative to life outside the labour market. Our society is organised on the basis of people having jobs. Marriage, families, homes, and even leisure activities all demand incomes which derive from employment. Without employment, these young people and others like them are effectively excluded from the mainstream of society.

Therefore, the implications of this study are simple and straightforward. Jobs will need to be found, and found soon, if many members of this generation of young people are not to be left behind permanently. In the short-term, such young people need counselling about seeking and finding work, including work on government schemes. They need advice and counselling about training and upgrading their skills. In the long-term, however, they need stable jobs. Measures will need to be taken to overcome the reluctance of employers to take on the long-term unemployed. Such measures might include subsidies and special schemes, as well as information to persuade them that there is considerable talent to exploit among this generation, despite their years of joblessness. Government has consistently recognised the special position of the young unemployed, but its measures to help them have been too little and too late for the age cohort from which this group of young people were drawn. Moreover, a danger exists that they will suffer further from being the guinea pigs for an inadequate Job Training Scheme. If effective ways of assisting this generation are not found, however, the young and jobless of this report may be condemned to remaining jobless when they are no longer young.

BIBLIOGRAPHY

Allen, G.A. *A Sociology of Friendship and Kinship,* London: George Allen and Unwin, 1979.

Ashton, D.N. *Unemployment under Capitalism,* London: Wheatsheaf Books, 1986.

Ashton, D.N. and Field, D. *Young Workers: The Transition from School to Work,* London: Hutchinson, 1976.

Ashton, D.N. and Maguire, M. *Young Adults in the Labour Market,* Department of Employment Research Paper No 55, n.d.

Banks M., Ullah, P. and Warr, P. Unemployment and less qualified urban young people, *Employment Gazette,* August 1984.

Banks, O. *Sociology of Education, Second Edition,* Batsford, London,1975.

Berthoud, R. *The Reform of Supplementary Benefits, Working Paper A,* London: PSI, 1984.

Brenner, M.H. Mortality and the National Economy: A Review and the Experience of England and Wales, *Lancet,* 2, 1979.

Brown, C. *Black and White Britain: The Third PSI Study,* London: Heinemann, 1984.

Brown, C. and Gay, P. *Racial Discrimination: 17 years after the Act,* London: PSI No. 646, 1985.

Cashmore, E.E. *No Future: Youth and Society,* London: Heinemann, 1984.

Casson, M. *Youth Unemployment,* London: Macmillan, 1979.

Chester, R. The Rise of the Neo-Conventional Family, *New Society,* 9 May 1985.

Clark, B.R. The cooling out function in higher education, *American Journal of Sociology,* 65, 1960.

Coffield, F., Borrill, C., and Marshall, S. *Growing up at the Margins,* Milton Keynes: Open University Press, 1986.

Cragg, A. and Dawson, T. *Unemployed Women: a study of attitudes and experiences,* London: Department of Employment Research Paper No. 47, 1984.

Daniel, W.W., Why is high unemployment still somehow acceptable?, *New Society,* 19 March 1981.

Daniel, W.W. and Stilgoe, E., *Where are They Now? A Follow-up Study of the Unemployed,* PEP Vol 63, No 572, October 1977.

Dahrendorf, R., The erosion of citizenship and its consequences for all of us, *New Statesman,* 12 June 1987.

Dex, S. *The Sexual Division of Work,* London: Wheatsheaf Books, 1985.

Dixon, K. Friendship and the Stability of Structural Inequality, mimeo, Simon Fraser University, 1976.

Economist Intelligence Unit, *Coping With Unemployment: The effects on the unemployed themselves,* December 1982.

Ethnic origin and economic status, *Employment Gazette,* January 1987.

European Economic Commission, *Chomage et Recherche d'un Emploi: attitudes et Dopinions des publics Europeens,* Brussels, 1979.

15 to 18, Report of the Central Advisory Council for Education — England. HMSO, 1959.

Fineman, S. *White-Collar Unemployment: Impact and Stress,* London: John Wiley, 1983.

Gravelle, H.S.E., Hutchison, G. and Stern, J. Mortality and unemployment: a cautionary note, Discussion Paper No. 95, *Centre for Labour Economics,* London School of Economics, 1981.

Half our Future, A report of the Central Advisory Council for Education (England), HMSO, 1971.

Halsey, A.H., Heath, A., and Ridge, J. *Origins and Destinations,* Oxford: Clarendon Press, 1980.

Hakim, C. The Social Consequences of High Unemployment, *Journal of Social Policy,* 11, 4, 1982.

Harrison, R. The demoralising experience of prolonged unemployment, *Department of Employment Gazette,* 84, 2, 1976.

Hutson, S., and Jenkins, R., Family Relationships and the Unemployment of young People in Swansea, forthcoming in *The Social World of the Young Unemployed,* Proceedings of a research seminar held at the Policy Studies Institue, London, 17 December 1986.

Jahoda, M., Lazarsfeld, P.F., and Zeisel, H. *Marienthal: The Sociography of an Unemployed Community* (English translation, 1972) London: Tavistock Publications, 1933.

Jarvie, I., *Rationality and Relativism: in search of a philosophy and history of anthropology,* London: Routledge Kegan Paul, 1984.

Komarovsky, M. *Unemployed Man and His Family: The Effect of Unemployment upon the Status of the Man in Fifty-Nine Families,* Arno, 1940.

Leonard, D. *Sex and Generation: A study of courtship and weddings,* London: Tavistock Publications, 1980.

McKee,L. and Bell, C. His Unemployment: Her Problem. The Domestic Consequences of Male Unemployment, paper given at British Sociological Association Annual Conference, 1984.

Madge, N. Unemployment and its Effect on Children, *Journal of Child Pyschology and Psychiatry*, 24, 2, 1983.

Manpower Services Commission, *Young People and Work*, 1977.

Marshall, G. On the sociology of women's unemployment, its neglect and significance, *Sociological Review*, 32, 2, 1984.

Martin, J. and Roberts, C. *Women and Employment: A lifetime perspective*, London: Department of Employment and Office of Population Censuses and Surveys, 1984.

Meade-King, M. Give or take another million *The Guardian*, 18 June 1986.

Miles, I. Is unemployment a health hazard? *New Scientist*, 12 May 1983.

Mills, C Wright *The Sociological Imagination*, New York: Oxford University Press, 1959.

Pahl, R.E. *Divisions of Labour*, Oxford: Basil Blackwell, 1984.

Payne, J. and Payne, C. Youth Unemployment 1974-81: The Changing Importance of Age and Qualifications, *Quarterly Journal of Social Affairs*, 1985.

Roberts, K. Contemporary Youth Unemployment: A Sociological Interpretation, paper presented to the British Association for the Advancement of Science, Annual Meeting September 1982.

Roberts, K. *Youth and Leisure*, London: George Allen & Unwin, 1983.

Roberts, K., Noble, M., and Duggan, J. Youth Unemployment: An Old Problem or a New Life-style? in K. Thompson (ed) *Work, Employment and Unemployment: Perspectives on Work and Society*, Milton Keynes: Open University Press, 1984.

Rose, R. *Getting by in Three Economies: The Resources of Official, Unofficial and Domestic Economies*, Centre for the Study of Public Policy, University of Strathclyde, 1983

Sinfield, A. Unemployment in an Unequal Society in B. Showler and A. Sinfield (eds) *The Workless State: Studies in Unemployment*, Oxford: Martin Robertson, 1981.

Smith, D.J. *Unemployment and Racial Minorities*, PSI, No. 594, February 1981.

Sorrentino, C. Unemployment in International Perspective in Showler and Sinfield (eds) *op cit*, 1981.

Taylor, M. Growing up without work: a study of young unemployed people in the West Midlands in *Growing Up Without Work: Two case studies*, Studies and Documents/4, European Centre for Work and Society, 1983.

Wells, W. *The relative pay and employment of young people,* Department of Employment Research Paper No. 42, 1983.

White, M. *Long-term Unemployment and Labour Markets,* London: PSI No. 622, 1983.

White, M. and McRae, S. *Long-term Unemployment among 18-24 Year Olds,* forthcoming, PSI.

Willis, P. Youth Unemployment: 1. A new social state, *New Society,* 29 March 1984.

Willis, P. Youth Unemployment: 2. Ways of Living, *New Society,* 5 April 1984.